GREAT TRAIN
ROBBERIES
OF THE
OLD WEST

GREAT TRAIN ROBBERIES OF THE OLD WEST

R. MICHAEL WILSON

TWODOT®

GUILFORD, CONNECTICUT
HELENA, MONTANA
AN IMPRINT OF THE GLOBE PEQUOT PRESS

A · T W O D O T® · B O O K

Text design by Lisa Reneson
Map by Melissa Baker © Morris Book Publishing, LLC
Spot art throughout by David Sylvester

Library of Congress Cataloging-in-Publication Data
Wilson, R. Michael, 1944-
  Great train robberies of the Old West / R. Michael Wilson. — 1st ed.
      p. cm.
  Includes bibliographical references and index.
  ISBN 978-0-7627-4150-2

  1. Train robberies—West (U.S.)—History. 2. Brigands and robbers—West (U.S.)—History. 3. Outlaws—West (U.S.)—History. I. Title.
  HV6661.W47W55 2007b
  364.15'52—dc22

                                                                    2006018312

Printed in the United States of America

10 9 8 7 6 5 4 3 2

CONTENTS

ACKNOWLEDGMENTS

No historical work of detail and accuracy can be written without the extensive support of many organizations and experts. *Great Train Robberies of the Old West* is no exception, and following is a list of those individuals and organizations who made this book possible:

American Medical Association; Arizona State Historical Society; Arizona Territorial Prison Historic State Park; Bancroft Library at Berkeley, California; Denver Public Library; Montana State Historical Society; National Archives and Record Administration; National Outlaw Lawman Association (NOLA); Nevada State Historical Society; Nevada State Archives; Roy Paul Odell, train robbery expert; New Mexico State Historical Society; Ohio State Historical Society; Oregon State Historical Society; Sharlot Hall Museum Archive; Tommy Shults, Railfan; University of Texas, Austin; Larry Walker of Magazine House; and the Wyoming State Archives.

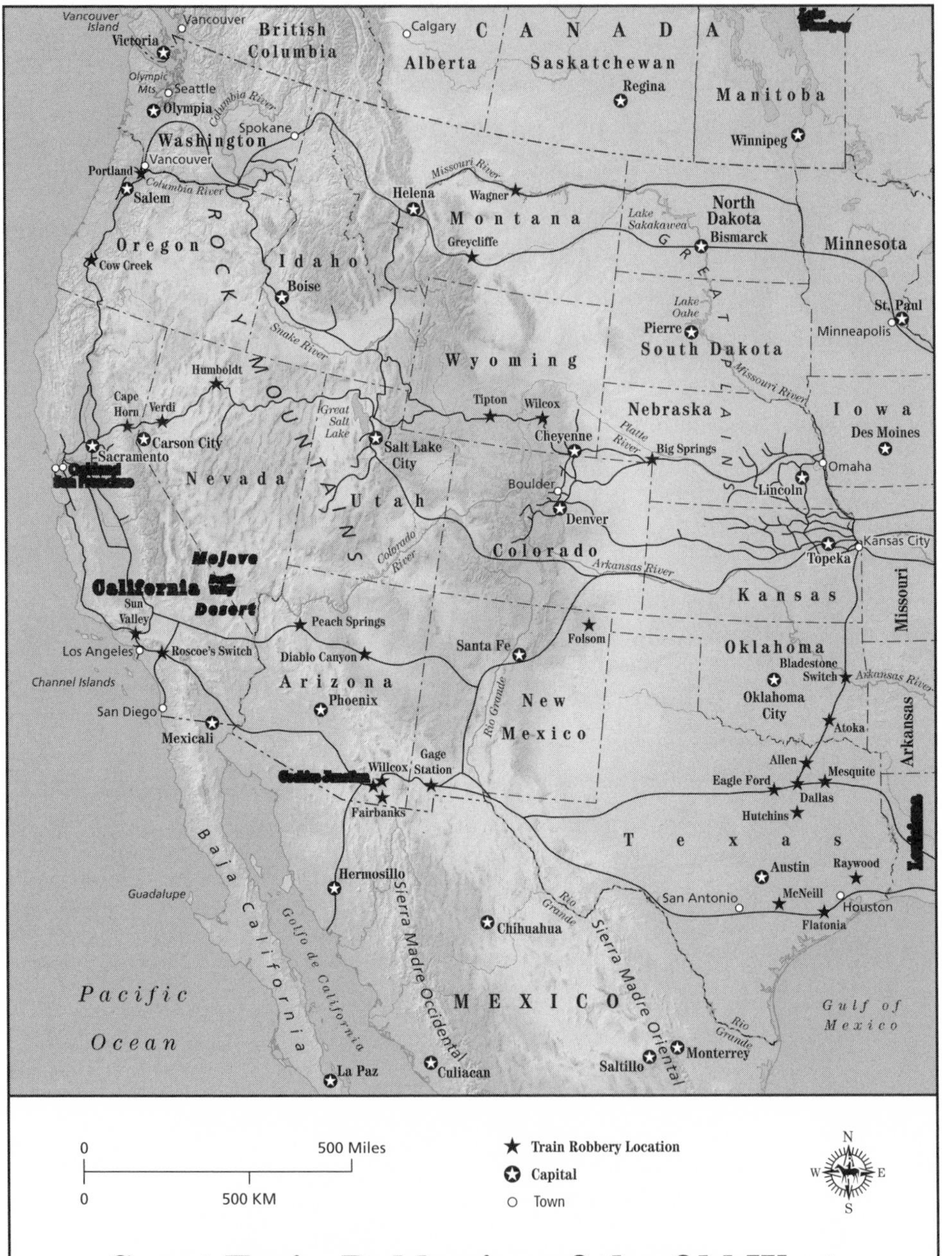

Vancouver Island
Vancouver
Victoria
British Columbia
Calgary
CANADA
Alberta
Saskatchewan
Regina
Manitoba
Winnipeg
Olympic Mts
Seattle
Olympia
Columbia River
Spokane
Washington
Vancouver
Portland
Salem
Columbia River
Missouri River
Helena
Wagner
Montana
Lake Sakakawea
North Dakota
Bismarck
Minnesota
Greycliffe
Oregon
Cow Creek
ROCKY MOUNTAINS
Idaho
Boise
GREAT PLAINS
Lake Oahe
St. Paul
Minneapolis
Pierre
South Dakota
Snake River
Wyoming
Missouri River
Humboldt
Cape Horn
Verdi
Tipton
Wilcox
Nebraska
Iowa
Des Moines
Great Salt Lake
Cheyenne
Platte River
Big Springs
Carson City
Sacramento
Salt Lake City
Omaha
Nevada
Boulder
Lincoln
Utah
Denver
Colorado River
Colorado
Kansas City
Topeka
Arkansas River
Mojave Desert
California
Kansas
Missouri
Sun Valley
Peach Springs
Folsom
Los Angeles
Roscoe's Switch
Santa Fe
Oklahoma
Diablo Canyon
Bladestone Switch
Arkansas River
Channel Islands
Arizona
Oklahoma City
Phoenix
New Mexico
Rio Grande
San Diego
Arkansas
Mexicali
Atoka
Gage Station
Allen
Willcox
Mesquite
Eagle Ford
Dallas
Fairbanks
Hutchins
Texas
Baja California
Austin
Raywood
Hermosillo
Sierra Madre Occidental
Rio Grande
Guadalupe
San Antonio
McNeill
Houston
Flatonia
Golfo de California
Chihuahua
Sierra Madre Oriental
Pacific Ocean
MEXICO
Gulf of Mexico
Rio Grande
Monterrey
Saltillo
Culiacan
La Paz
0
500 Miles
0
500 KM
Train Robbery Location
Capital
Town
N
W
E
S

Great Train Robberies of the Old West

INTRODUCTION

The history of trains and the history of train robbery in the Old West both had their roots in the entrepreneurial spirit that characterized westward expansion. The first railroad built by an American in the United States was completed in 1809 by John Thompson in Pennsylvania. It was a mere three-quarters of a mile in length and was designed to carry stone from the quarry of Thomas Leiper just south of Swarthmore to Ridley Creek in Chester. On February 28, 1827, the Baltimore and Ohio Railroad incorporated to establish America's first line to carry passengers as well as freight. It collected its inaugural passenger fare on January 7, 1830. The passenger business had such potential that the B&O, on July 4, 1831, introduced passenger cars with a center aisle to make boarding and seating more accommodating.

The first railroad west of the Mississippi River was the Pacific Railway of Missouri, which incorporated on March 12, 1840, but this railroad did not have a test run until December 9, 1852. Two weeks later the Pacific Railway began regular passenger service. The interest in building railroads increased steadily before the Civil War; but, to further encourage track laying, railroads were designated "post roads," and lucrative contracts for carrying the mails were awarded.

The U.S. Congress saw the need for a railroad across the country for mail and military purposes and chartered the Army Topographic Corps to conduct surveys as early as 1853. The most northern route was between the forty-seventh and forty-ninth parallels. Conducted under Isaac Ingalls Stevens, then governor of Washington Territory, this survey followed the route proposed as early as 1849 by Asa Whitney, one of the first backers of a transcontinental railroad. Another party, under an ill-fated Captain John W. Gunnison, explored the route along the thirty-eighth and thirty-ninth parallels. When his party was massacred by Indians, the survey was continued along the forty-first parallel by Lieutenant E. G. Beckwith. A route along the Mexican border, the thirty-fifth parallel, was surveyed by Captain A. W. Whipple and Lieutenant J. C. Ives.

Because all four of these routes seemed feasible, a controversy arose over whether to establish the line in the north or the south, delaying the start of the Pacific Railroad for a decade. A fifth survey, conducted at this same time under Lieutenant Robert S. Williamson in the West, ran north and south and was intended to connect the Washington and Oregon Territories with California and the Pacific Railroad.

In 1856 the first western railroad on the Pacific coast, a mere 17 miles of track, was built in the Sacramento Valley under the supervision of civil engineer Theodore D. Judah. He was a man of vision who saw the possibilities offered by a railroad originating in California and continuing on to Nebraska, where it would connect with railroads to the East. The Central Pacific Railroad of California Company was incorporated on June 28, 1861, for that purpose. When government support was sought, however, President Abraham Lincoln responded, "Private enterprise must build the Pacific Railroad. All government can do is aid, even admitting its construction is a political as well as a military necessity."

The Pacific Railroad Act, which passed on July 1, 1862, empowered the Central Pacific to build eastward from Sacramento while the newly chartered Union Pacific Railroad was charged with the responsibility to build westward from Nebraska.

The original place chosen for the tracks to connect was located in Nevada. The westbound Union Pacific Railroad faced a great deal of flat, open land with only four tunnels to build. The eastbound Central Pacific Railroad had to traverse the Sierra Nevada mountain range with many tunnels to bore and numerous rock faces to cut away to form a railroad bed. However, the western company was using thousands of Chinese laborers who did not cause any significant labor problems, and supplies were kept readily available through the port at San Francisco and carried up river to the train depot at Sacramento. The Union Pacific Railroad, in contrast, was using primarily Irish immigrants who caused delays and stoppages, and supplies became difficult to obtain once the tracks progressed beyond the Missouri River.

The final delay was caused by the Union Pacific workers over pay issues and came on the very day the tracks were first scheduled to connect. All these Union Pacific difficulties caused the place of connection to move eastward as the Central Pacific continued to lay track after crossing the mountains, until the location to meet was finally established at Promontory Point in Utah.

The tracks of the two railroads officially joined on May 10, 1869, allowing trains to begin operating coast to coast. From California the eastward tracks of the Pacific Railroad scaled the Sierra Nevadas and dropped into the Nevada desert, soon passing through the station at Verdi, Nevada, with "tea kettle" steam engines pulling express, baggage, and mail cars, supplanting stagecoaches as a main carrier of treasure. In a few years the Pacific Railroad would come to be known as the Transcontinental Railroad.

Train robbery was a unique American experience for the last quarter of the nineteenth century. By the end of 1870, several trains had been robbed east of the Mississippi River, but no one had tried to rob a western train. In the West the distance between towns, stations, and water stops was great and the land through which the tracks were laid was often quite desolate. Robbing a stagecoach, though risky, seemed manageable to road agents as the number of people aboard could not exceed twenty-one—usually average citizens, excepting the occasional bold shotgun messenger. Trains, on the other hand, traveled such long distances that the passengers could not be screened by the robbers' agents. Trains could carry more than a hundred passengers, any of whom could be as hard a case as any of the robbers, or a capable lawman, a cantankerous military man, or an ornery cowboy. Trains were large and powerful, and steam power was somewhat of a mystery in comparison to a six-horse team. Still, once the trains started carrying the treasures of the West, it was just a matter of time before someone tried to rob one.

A couple of times in the mid-1860s, men in the East had broken into an unoccupied express car and thrown out the safe, but this was a burglary of a rail car rather than a robbery. It wasn't until October 6, 1866, that the Reno brothers committed the first post-war robbery of a train in motion. The Ohio & Mississippi Railroad's passenger train was traveling northeast from St. Louis, Missouri, to Cincinnati, Ohio, when the train was boarded and robbed near Seymour, Indiana. Early on the morning of December 12, 1868, the Reno brothers and two other members of their gang were hanged at New Albany, Indiana. It was hoped that this example would put an end to train robbery.

When train robberies continued, there was a call to set the penalty for the offense at death and make it a federal crime, but it would be three decades before the U.S. Congress would act. The successes of train robbers in the East, however, would prove relatively insignificant in comparison to that line of work in the West. By the early 1870s there were thousands of miles of track laid west of the Mississippi River. The express cars carried gold, silver, and the other mineral wealth from the many mines of the West, as well as rich payrolls to keep those mines operating. Trains had not replaced stagecoaches but, rather, often accumulated the smaller quantities of the treasure transported by the coaches and forwarded it in a single large shipment.

On November 5, 1870, the Central Pacific's No. 1 train was robbed near Verdi Station, Nevada, as you will learn in Chapter 1. Five men

Train robbers frequently used the "blind baggage"
car to climb aboard the train.
JOSEPHINE COUNTY HISTORICAL SOCIETY

boarded while the train was stopped with two of the men taking over the engine at gunpoint. They forced the engineer to bring the train to a halt in an isolated location. There, the engine, tender, and express cars, which were almost always coupled just behind the tender, were uncoupled from the rest of the train and pulled a distance farther down the track where the express car, under the supervision of Central Pacific's express agent Frank Marshall, was robbed. Jack Davis led the gang, but a man named Chapman had planned the robbery. Even though he used the same plan first devised by the Reno brothers and used several times after 1866, it has often been called the Chapman Plan or, after the Big Springs, Nebraska, robbery in 1877, the Collins Plan.

The Chapman method followed the *modus operandi* of the stage-coach robbers—finding a place where the train was stopped or slowed so it could be boarded and the robbers could take control. It relied upon boarding at the "blind baggage" platform located at the front of the express car, aptly named because there was no way to see if anyone had come aboard there. This location allowed robbers to board and wait until they reached their chosen location before climbing over the tender and getting the drop on the engineer and fireman. Once in control of the engine, they were free to conduct their robbery as they saw fit. A later development of the Chapman Plan was to stop the train on a trestle before the engine, tender, and express cars were uncoupled and driven forward, thus keeping the passengers from exiting and interfering. Twelve hours after the first western train robbery, another gang of robbers missed their chance when they robbed the same train and the same express car, under the supervision of the same agent, Frank Marshall, at Pequop, Nevada.

The second method of robbing trains, wrecking for robbery, was particularly offensive to the public because it could be quite costly in the loss of life and property. This method was first used on October 11, 1866, when four men loosened a rail, attached a wire, and pulled the rail away just as the Louisville & Nashville train approached Briscoe Station, Kentucky. They intended to wreck the entire train for the purpose of robbing it, but because the engineer acted quickly, only the engine, tender, and express car were derailed. Still, this was enough for the men, who were never identified, to get away with more than $8,000, an equal amount having been hidden before they gained entry. Jesse James adopted this method when he wrecked a train at Adair, Iowa, on July 21, 1873, and the train wreck method has sometimes been called the James method of train robbery.

The first attempt at wrecking a train for robbery in the West was made by "Big Nose" George Parrott at Medicine Bow, Wyoming, in June 1878, but an alert crew spotted the loose rail and fixed it before the train arrived. It would not be until August 31, 1881, at Cape Horn, California, that the first western train was wrecked to commit a robbery.

Various methods were devised to thwart train robbers. It had been suggested that moving the express and baggage cars to a different place in the line of train cars might discourage robbers, but after careful consideration it was decided always to couple the express and mail cars behind the tender. It was proposed that a window be placed at the front of the express and mail cars so messengers could see onto the "blind baggage" platform, but it was concluded that this would only provide a new place for robbers to easily gain entry into the car, or at least thrust their guns through the window and force the agent to open the door.

During the heyday of robberies, one messenger, recognizing that most robberies occurred at night, invented the Eradicator, a basket beneath the express car connected by an L-shaped gas pipe into which the express car agent inserted a railroad flare. Once the flare fell into the basket it would light up the entire area around the car, but there is no record of the Eradicator ever being used. Later in the evolution of train robbery, railroads began to dispatch "specials" with mounted posses, reducing the time robbers had to escape and increasing the likelihood of capture and recovery of their plunder. Even the increased risk of capture, however, had little effect on deterrence.

When nothing strategic or mechanical seemed to stop the robberies, it was thought that legislation might be the answer. If train robbery were a capital offense, it was suggested, robbers would not take the risk. However, when California passed a death-penalty bill in 1891, the rate of train robberies actually increased. Many of the state and territorial laws for train robbery were so poorly worded that convictions were easily overturned on appeal. Furthermore, juries were not inclined to return a verdict of guilty, which could result in the accused's execution, if no one was killed during the robbery. When it was proposed that a federal death penalty law was the answer, William Pinkerton of Pinkerton's Detective Agency said, "If it becomes a crime against the United States government to hold up a train, it is almost certain that this class of work will soon come to an end."

The first effort to pass a train robbery bill failed in 1893. Interest waned as the country fell into a depression, but robberies continued until nine years later when the U.S. Congress finally passed the Train Robbery Act. By then, however, other developments had made train robbery a less inviting profession. Most of the western mines had played out, the treasure carried on the trains had decreased, and treasure was not sent on any regular schedule, making it quite difficult to plan a train robbery. Even the booty that could be collected from passengers had all but disappeared as currency and coin had been replaced by traveler's checks, an alternative devised by the American Express Company in 1891. As there was simply nothing to steal from a train that was worth the effort and the risk, train robberies after the turn of the century became rare, but there were a few diehard train robbers still plying their trade well into the 1920s.

One of the greatest obstacles for lawmen to overcome was the sympathy shown to train robbers in the West as a result of the animosity felt toward the railroads at the time. The railroads had promised cheap land to those who settled upon the vast tracts granted by the government along their right of way. However, when it came time to sell the improved land, the prices increased, often out of reach for the poor settlers. The result was that many were evicted from the land where they had cultivated fields, built homes, and raised families. The railroads also had a practice of arbitrarily setting shipping fees high, thus cutting deeply into the profits of the ranchers and farmers. The railroads cut their way through lands that had been open range, claiming the surrounding land as theirs. Knowing that the route they chose in laying their tracks could make a prosperous town or a ghost town, they used this tactic to punish towns that had not cooperated with their demands.

Anyone who hurt the railroad was a hero and earned the respect and support of a substantial portion of the population. When train robbers were eluding lawmen, they could count on being harbored and supplied by farmers and ranchers and could always find fresh horses to make their escape.

Even when a robber was jailed, he would soon break out of the flimsy structures and be free to rob again or live comfortably for a while on his plunder. Some of that plunder was buried in order to be recovered later, and the stories of loot still buried are numerous.

In all there were nearly a thousand train robberies and failed or abandoned attempts to rob trains between 1866 and 1910. Only a few of these, however, rise to the level of greatness because of the amount stolen, the brutality or bravado of the robbers, the ingenuity of the train-men, the persistence of the lawmen, or the circumstances of the robbery and its aftermath. In the pages that follow, you will read about a few of these exceptional criminal adventures.

The first in a long series of related events always holds a place of special prominence, but the first western train robbery was a landmark event because it established a method of operation which would be copied for nearly four decades. The robbery of Central Pacific's Overland Express at Verdi, Nevada, in November 1871 produced more than $40,000 for the six robbers, but the men never had the chance to spend their ill-gotten loot.

Many train-robbing gangs started in other lines of work, with stagecoach robbery at the top of that list. However, when stagecoach robbery proved unprofitable, the gangs naturally graduated to train rob-bery. In 1877 the Collins gang abandoned Deadwood and the stage routes for the railroads of Nebraska and assaulted a Union Pacific train at Big Springs. Four of the robbers were killed, their share of the loot recovered, but two robbers fled into Texas and returned to that line of work that paid best—robbing trains.

Sam Bass learned the art of train robbing from Joel Collins in Nebraska and took what he learned into Texas. He formed his gang, tried robbing stagecoaches, and quickly confirmed what he had learned in Deadwood: Train robbing paid well while stagecoach robbery did not. He robbed the first train in Texas's history, and three more before a bullet stopped him.

The first train wrecked for robbery occurred only a few days after the first train was robbed in America. Still it took more than a decade before anyone would try to wreck a western train, and three more years before a train was actually derailed for robbery. When the train left the tracks at Cape Horn, all the robbers had to do was gather their booty, but they lost their nerve and fled empty-handed.

Train robbers were colorful characters, none more so than Kit Joy who has been described as a "half-blind, one-legged, toothless bandit."

After the Joy gang robbed a train, two members were shot down by the pursuing posse and two more were lynched after they killed a posse member. Only Joy survived because he fled, but he was captured and lived to serve a long prison term.

Jay Gould became one of the most despised railroad millionaires in America, especially in the southwest. When a gang formed to assault Gould's trains, and took only Gould's money, they were celebrated as heroes and supported by the local citizens.

Four cowboys, starved for excitement and anxious to make a big haul, robbed a train at Canyon Diablo, Arizona. The robbery yielded one of the most thrilling pursuits in the history of the Old West. The posse, led by American war hero Bucky O'Neill, got its men.

Two men twice robbed Southern Pacific's No. 20 northbound train at Roscoe's Station, California. During the second robbery the train was derailed and two men were killed. While robbery was one matter, brutal murder was quite another, and lawmen relentlessly tracked down the robbers and lodged them in jail. Although California had made train robbery a capital offense, and first-degree murder had always been punishable by death, both men were sentenced only to long prison terms.

Nathaniel "Texas Jack" Reed formed a gang to rob the Katy No. 2 train at Blackstone Switch, Oklahoma. The gang never gained entrance to the express car and took less than $500 in currency, watches, and pistols from the passengers. A Deputy U.S. Marshal was later killed trying to make an arrest, and this outraged the citizens and motivated lawmen. Four men were arrested but the other robber fled the territory and was not heard of again. One of the four men arrested was acquitted, one turned state's evidence and was released, one died in a federal prison, and the leader served less than a year behind prison walls.

Train robbers set giant powder cartridges on the tracks at Cow Creek, Oregon, but the explosives did not derail the train and were mistaken for warning torpedoes. The robbers failed to open the safe, got only $1,000 from the mails, and finally had to go through the passengers to get another $500. Three men were arrested, but one was acquitted.

The other two men were convicted, but after their case was overturned on appeal they were released.

Two men robbed Atlantic & Pacific's train near Peach Springs, Arizona, but one was killed and the other fled with only a few packages from the registered mail pouch. The train robber was captured and lodged in Prescott's jail, but during an escape Fleming "Jim" Parker murdered County Attorney Lee Norris. Parker was sentenced to death for the murder and expiated his crime on the gallows.

The Wild Bunch, in their Hole in the Wall redoubt, often numbered 150 desperate men but fewer than a dozen men were involved in the train-robbing business. The train robbers used explosives liberally and typically blew the express cars into splinters, often shredding and burning their plunder. The two leaders, Butch Cassidy and the Sundance Kid, fled to South America and were never prosecuted for their American crimes.

Tom and Sam Ketchum formed a gang and assaulted trains in Texas and New Mexico at the turn of the century. Tom Ketchum became infamous when he tried to rob a train single-handed, became the only man in the Old West hanged for a crime other than first degree murder, and was beheaded during the most bungled execution on record.

Every "great" train robbery involved, at some point, a dedicated and capable lawman. The robbery of a train at Cochise Junction, Arizona, in September 1899, and later another at Fairbanks, was notable because a lawman was leader of the train robbers and used his position to misdirect the investigation. Constable Burt Alvord eluded capture for several years, but finally made a deal to capture murderer Augustine Chacon in return for a minimum sentence. However, he was reluctant to serve even two years behind prison walls and escaped. Alvord remained free for several more years before he was captured and delivered to the notorious Arizona Territorial Prison near Yuma.

CHAPTER ONE

THE FIRST TRAIN ROBBERY IN THE WEST

John E. Chapman was a quiet man—a schoolteacher, religious leader, and respectable citizen of Reno, Nevada—before he made the acquaintance of A. J. "Gentleman Jack" Davis. Gentleman Jack was the wealthy owner of a prosperous mill in Six-Mile Canyon. He was charming and witty and well thought of in the community, so he was a constant member of the best social circles, but Davis also had among his friends some men of the most questionable character in the vicinity, including R. A. "Sol" Jones, James Gilchrist, E. B. Parsons, Tilton P. Cockerill, John Squiers, and Chat Roberts. This gang, which had been involved in stagecoach robberies in northwestern Nevada but never suspected, saw that the days of finding a fortune on a stagecoach were quickly passing because the large treasure hauls were now carried in the express cars of the railroads.

The group met at Chat Roberts's ranch where Chapman, at Davis's urging, devised a plan to capture the treasure from a train using the general *modus operandi* employed in robbing stagecoaches—finding a place where the train was naturally stopped or slowed to allow boarding and then taking control of the engine, tender, express, and baggage cars.

Since Chapman was too weak, or too inexperienced in the ways of the road agent, to participate in a train robbery, he was sent to San Francisco where he was to watch for a big shipment. Chapman must have had, or somehow acquired, knowledge of railroad and Wells, Fargo & Co. operations because he knew that the code words "Red Coat" meant a big payroll shipment for the Gold Hill mines. Under his alias of Joseph Enrique, Chapman sent a ciphered telegram to Jones saying that the Central Pacific Overland Express had pulled out of San Francisco with a payroll of $60,000 in gold aboard. Chapman had done his part and earned a share of the plunder.

Jones spread the word among his fellow gang members, and then the six men saddled up for the ride to an abandoned mine in the Peavine Mountains, not far from Verdi but 11 miles west of Reno. It was raining hard in the lower elevations, and the rain had turned to heavy snows in the higher altitudes of the Sierras. As the train passed through Verdi just after midnight on November 5, 1870, it slowed. As it passed a shed, five men wearing black masks and dusters swung aboard—three on the "blind baggage" platform between the tender and the combination express baggage car, and two on the rear platform of the same car where it was coupled to the remainder of the train. Two of the men at the front of the car climbed over the tender, pistols cocked, and took engineer Hank Small and his fireman prisoner. The third man at the front of the car, seeing that the engine had been secured, climbed over the roof of the express car to the rear platform and informed the two men stationed there of their success in taking control of the train.

Conductor Marshall was working his way toward the engine. When he stepped from the first passenger car onto the rear platform of the express car, he was confronted by three men pointing six-shooters at him; he retreated and locked the door behind him. The engineer, at that moment, was being forced to "whistle off the brakes," which required brakemen to go to their stations and prepare to bring the train to a halt by mechanically applying the brakes. The engineer gave the required single short blast of his whistle, which also signaled the men at the rear of the express baggage car to pull the pin to uncouple the rest of the train and cut the bell rope. This having been done, the engine, tender, and express baggage car continued down the tracks while the rest of the train screeched to a halt several miles east of Verdi. When the engine reached the Lawton Springs gravel quarry, where Jones waited with six saddle horses and two packhorses, the engineer was ordered to stop at the barricade of rail ties piled on the tracks. This brought the train to a halt at the precise place the robbers wanted.

The engineer and fireman were herded as a shield to the express car where engineer Small was ordered to knock and ask to be admitted. Central Pacific's express messenger Frank Minch did not arm himself because he recognized Small's voice and opened the sliding door to the express car. Covered by three sawed-off double-barreled shotguns—one right in his face—he immediately surrendered. The robbers had the engineer and fireman climb into the car and join the messenger, who was facing the wall. The robbers searched for treasure while Jones brought forward tools to pry off the padlocks on the boxes, and the work was begun. They found one treasure box contained silver dollars by spilling out one bag, and then ignored that chest as they looked for the gold. It took an hour to search the car, and their take—$41,000 in $20 gold pieces—was short of the $60,000 they expected. They left behind over $8,000 in silver bars and coins, which were too heavy to carry for their value, and ignored piles of bank drafts and other negotiable papers. Somehow they had overlooked $15,000 in gold bars buried beneath the woodpile. These, with their plunder and the silver, would have totaled more than the anticipated $60,000.

Davis made a careful inspection of the car to see that no clues were left behind before departing from the train.

The party of robbers moved some distance away into the quarry where the loot, weighing close to 150 pounds, was divided and placed into the saddlebags of the horses. Davis took about half of the coins with the other five men getting an equal share of the remainder. It was the responsibility of the leader to see that Chapman got his share from the

George Downey.
Chief of Police.

B. F. Lackey.
Officer.

R. A. Jones.

James Gilchrist.

C. T. Roberts.

Tilton Cockerell.

John Squeers.

A. J. Davis,
Chief of Band.

J. H. Chapman.

Sketch of the Verdi train robbery and photos of the major players
NEVADA HISTORICAL SOCIETY, RENO

$20,000 he had packed onto the two packhorses, and he started out alone. The other five men separated into two parties and each headed in a different direction. Jones and Cockerill left together toward Reno while Squiers, Parsons, and Gilchrist headed northwest toward California. The men had left behind at the quarry a crowbar and sawed-off shotgun, but these items provided no clues to their identity.

Conductor Marshall coordinated the careful release of the brakes on the passenger cars, and the train rolled ahead down the gentle grade until it reached the engine, tender, and express car. He stopped the rear of the train a safe distance back. After the obstruction was removed, the train was coupled together. It was then backed into Verdi where the engineer planned to send a telegram to Charley Pegg, the sheriff at the county seat of Washoe City, but he discovered that the wires had been cut. The train then proceeded to Reno to report the robbery, arriving at dawn at about the same time the telegraph lines were repaired. Sheriff Pegg and Undersheriff J. H. Kinkead formed a posse, and sixteen men took the field. Pegg's information was faulty, so he ended up spending valuable time following a false trail. By the time they realized their error and returned to Washoe City, Wells, Fargo & Company had posted a reward of $10,000. The Central Pacific Railroad and the state of Nevada quickly added $15,000 each, bringing the total reward for arrest and conviction of the six robbers to $40,000.

Since all three parties had an interest in the case and all agreed to share manpower and resources, they put F. T. Burke, the most experienced detective, in charge. He examined the scene and found tracks, one from a distinctive "gambler's boot," a narrow shoe with an unusually small heel. He followed the track for several hundred yards where it left the hard ground of the rails. There he found two other foot tracks and the place where three men mounted horses and headed north toward Dog Valley Creek in Sardine Valley, California. Burke's posse followed the tracks and finally came to Pearson's Tavern, where they found the proprietor sitting with his shotgun across his lap, waiting for California lawmen to arrive.

Pearson said his wife had discovered that one of their boarders had a large number of gold coins. They suspected he might be a brigand of some sort, but his two partners had departed the day before. The men approached the room with the greatest stealth and had Mrs. Pearson knock. When the occupant opened the door, he looked into the muzzles of several rifles and pistols, so he had no opportunity to resist. He was handcuffed and questioned.

It was learned his name was James Gilchrist, who was known to some posse members as an unskilled mine laborer from Virginia City. Gilchrist's flippant demeanor suggested he would not break easily, so Sheriff Pegg let slip that the people were so outraged by this first robbery of a western train that a large lynch mob was forming at that moment. The prisoner weakened and began to talk, naming the others involved in the robbery, but he could only say that Parsons and Squiers were heading for Loyalton in Sierra Valley and from there were planning to go on to a hideout in Grass Valley. He knew nothing of the whereabouts of the other men. Pegg sent a telegram to Reno to have Davis and Chapman arrested as soon as they appeared in town, and the posse then started after Parsons and Squiers, Gilchrist's companions.

Upon arriving in Loyalton, the posse discovered that there was only one hotel in the tiny town, so Burke and Pegg went there to ask about strangers. The proprietor said that there was only one stranger staying there and he was in room 21, but his description did not match the man described by Gilchrist or Mrs. Pearson. Still, they decided they should see the man before they dismissed him as one of the robbers. They found the door to room 21 warped and held shut by a leaning chair. Burke reached inside and moved the chair away carefully. The posse entered with rifles and shotguns at the ready and found the occupant sleeping soundly. They removed his loaded revolver from beneath his pillow and, upon wakening him, they found they had captured Parsons, a gambler from Virginia City who wore a "gambler's boot."

After the prisoner was secured in double shackles and on his way to the jail at Truckee, Pegg learned that Squiers's brother had a ranch a few miles from town. He and his posse rode there before daylight. They surrounded the farmhouse to await the appearance of Squiers. Within a few minutes a man came out to milk the cow and left the door ajar. The entire posse slipped into the house and found Squiers asleep in his bedroll, with eight other men also sleeping on the floor. They captured Squiers but nearly had to fight the occupants and neighbors, who all agreed that the posse had no authority to make an arrest in California. However, before the residents of Loyalton could organize and rescue the prisoner, the posse was able to obtain a buckboard and spirit him away. They lodged him in the Truckee jail with Gilchrist and Parsons and only had to wait one day to get their extradition order from Nevada's Governor Henry G. Blasdel, who had requisitioned it from California's Governor Henry H. Haight. Gilchrist, Parsons, and Squiers were returned to Washoe City and lodged in the Washoe County jail.

Before leaving Truckee, Gilchrist, in an effort to secure his freedom, had agreed to cooperate fully with the officers and told them where they had hidden those shares of the gold that were not found in their pockets. Judge T. Plunkett of Truckee City, J. J. Green, and James Eddington took Gilchrist to a spot 3 miles down the Honey Lake Road and then left the road some distance down a canyon. They stopped at a rugged ledge of rocks jutting out into the ravine where there was a natural cleft, into which the men had poured their gold coins. They succeeded in pulling out nearly $12,000 that day but returned the following day with the proper tools and recovered the remainder of the plunder, worth more than $750. Gilchrist also told the whereabouts of Davis's stash, though how he would know that is a mystery since he was not with Davis when he hid his share. However, Davis had already given up his gold coins to Chief of Police George W. Downey before the Truckee lawmen could go for them.

When Davis appeared in town, he was closely watched until all was ready. Then Officer Morrow stepped up to Davis "and nailed him." When told that the officers had caught some of the men engaged in the train robbery, Davis said, "I'll bet you $2.50 that you haven't."

Chief Downey answered, "I'll bet you $2.50 that I have one of them right here in town."

Davis asked, "Where?" and Downey pointed his finger at Davis and said, "There!"

Davis at first would not believe that any of his men had "peached," but the officers seemed so confident and had so many clues that he finally had to admit they knew enough. He decided he had better cooperate as well. He told the officers he would take them to where a great deal of the plunder was stashed and insisted he had not been involved in the robbery, but had only overheard men talking about the hiding place. He went with Chief Downey and two deputies to Hunter's Bridge on the Truckee River. Davis guided them to a place 100 yards above the bridge and the same distance from the railroad tracks and directed their attention to a clump of four sagebrush, saying the gold was beneath one of them. After Downey scuffed his boots in the loose dirt beneath one bush and kicked up gold coins, the tedious process of digging and collecting the coins proceeded until they had recovered nearly all of the $20,000 from the hole.

Davis, Parsons, Gilchrist, and Squiers were soon joined in the Washoe County jail by Jones, Cockerill, and Roberts, who had been tracked to a bordello in Long Valley by a heavily armed posse of twenty-eight men and arrested without resistance. Roberts had not taken part in the robbery and made a deal to testify. Meanwhile, Chapman, who had no idea that the scheme had been exposed and that he had been implicated, calmly disembarked from the Oakland to Reno stagecoach right into the arms of waiting lawmen. After all eight men were behind bars, people began to question certain circumstances in the region. It was then supposed, for example, that Davis had acquired the mill for the sole purpose of altering stolen bullion. From this, it was deduced that he must be involved in the many stagecoach robberies that had occurred in the vicinity over the previous six years. The confessions of several of the gang proved this true, but they were never prosecuted for those crimes.

A grand jury was convened by Judge C. N. Harris of the district court of Washoe County in late 1870, and all eight men were indicted for the train robbery. They were all found guilty, but Gilchrist and Roberts were released in consideration of turning state's evidence, while the other six men were sentenced to hard labor in the Nevada state penitentiary near Carson City. Squiers was sentenced to twenty-three years and was pardoned on April 10, 1882. Cockerill received twenty-two years and was pardoned on July 12, 1882. Chapman got twenty years and was pardoned on July 13, 1877. Parsons received eighteen years and, though involved in several escapes including the "Big Break" of 1871, was pardoned on November 7, 1881. Davis received ten years and was pardoned February 16, 1875. Jones was sentenced to six years and was pardoned on March 27, 1874. All the prisoners arrived at the prison between December 17 and December 25, 1870. After their release, all the train robbers disappeared from Nevada's criminal records except Davis.

Davis was a model prisoner during the first months of his imprisonment and that might have helped reduce his sentence by a small number of months, but on September 17, 1871, there was the "Big Break" at the Nevada state prison. The break occurred during the evening lockup when twelve of the most desperate prisoners broke into the armory and took control of all the prison's arms. Several guards were killed and two wounded, and Matt Pixley, a citizen responding to help the guards, was also killed. The dozen escapees opened all the cell doors and invited the other prisoners to join them, and seventeen did, but Davis refused to take part and even provided assistance to the guards. When Davis came up for his pardon hearing in December 1874, after serving only four years, the board took into consideration his help during the prison riot and recommended favorably for his release. The governor pardoned Davis on February 16, 1875.

Davis, though he seemed to have reformed, was committed to a life of crime. He assembled a small gang consisting of Bob Hamilton and Thomas Lauria and returned to the stage-robbing business. On September 3, 1877, three masked road agents stepped from the brush and tried to stop the stagecoach traveling between Eureka and Tybo. There was treasure on board, so the company had assigned shotgun messengers Eugene Blair and Jimmy Brown to ride along for protection. As soon as the road agents appeared, both messengers opened fire, Blair firing both barrels of his double-barreled shotgun at Davis. The gunfire was returned by Hamilton and Lauria. Davis had been riddled with buckshot, which killed him instantly, and messenger Brown received a wound in his leg. The other road agents fled but were soon captured, tried, convicted, and sentenced on December 8, 1877, to serve fourteen years in Nevada's state prison.

CHAPTER TWO

THE COLLINS GANG

Joel Collins was drawn into a life of crime by Sam Bass, but turned the tables on Bass and took control of the gang of robbers near Deadwood, Dakota Territory. He learned quickly that there was little money to be made in highway robbery so he guided five of his men, including Bass, south into Nebraska to rob a train. They made their assault at Big Springs, and just about when it looked like another "water haul" they found $60,000 in newly minted $20 gold coins. Collins had organized the robbery well, but he had overlooked the most important part of the play—the getaway.

Sam Bass was born in Lawrence County, Indiana, on July 21, 1851, the fourth of ten children. Because his mother died when he was 10 years old and his father passed on four years later, their eight children were distributed among relatives. Bass was taken in by his uncle, David Sheets of Lawrence County, and lived with him over the next five years. He worked on Sheets's farm and spent little time in school, so he remained illiterate. When he was nearly nineteen, Bass left home and traveled to St. Louis, Missouri, but quickly moved on to Rosedale, Mississippi. In 1872 Bass quit his job in the Rosedale sawmill and traveled to Denton, Texas, where he settled. He found employment herding cattle and driving

A staged train robbery
DENVER PUBLIC LIBRARY, WESTERN HISTORY COLLECTION, Z-2991

wagons on the ranch of Sheriff William F. "Dad" Egan. In late 1874 Bass bought a sorrel mare and soon discovered that she could run very fast, so he entered her in a few races and won easily. By March 1875, when horse racing began to interfere with his work, Egan issued an ultimatum to dispose of the horse or quit his job. Bass, who had always been a hard worker and dependable, chose to keep the horse.

Soon the reputation of the sorrel mare spread and, to find races, Bass had to travel some distance. He went into the Indian Territory where his mare ran and won a number of times. Since his winnings consisted mostly of ponies that the bettors were reluctant to part with, Bass waited patiently for the right moment, then gathered up the herd containing his stake ponies, and took along the rest of the animals as "interest" on the unpaid bets. He drove the herd to San Antonio, Texas, and sold them in December 1875. By then, only nine months after his leaving the employ of Sheriff Egan, Bass's life was firmly fixed in dissipation—horse racing, drinking, gambling, brawling, and horse stealing.

Bass met Joel Collins in San Antonio and quickly corrupted his new friend. Collins and his three brothers—Joe, Billy, and Henry—were born of good Kentucky stock. Collins's family had moved to Dallas early in Texas history, and by 1877 was one of the best families in that part of the state. The boys were all well educated and raised to be law-abiding gentlemen.

In December 1875 Collins lived in San Antonio and engaged in the stock raising and cattle trading business in the southwest part of the state but also owned a half interest in a San Antonio saloon. After Bass and Collins went on an extended spree, Collins sold his interest in the saloon and formed a partnership with Bass. They arranged a scheme where Bass represented himself as a horse trainer and in that capacity was able to time the various local race horses that might compete with his mare. When he was certain that his horse would win a race between the animals, he would encourage the owner to challenge Joel Collins, who was then representing himself as the owner of the mare. In this way they never lost a race and were able to accumulate a substantial stake to finance their wild ways, but they squandered the money almost as fast as they earned it.

By August 1876 they had played out their scam in Texas and decided to take what money remained and buy a herd of cattle, drive it to a Kansas market to sell, and take a fine profit. Relying in part on Collins's previous good reputation, they obtained a herd of 500 head of cattle, paying part in cash and contracting to pay the remainder after the cattle were sold. With Jack Davis they drove the herd into Kansas and sold it for $5,000. Instead of returning home and paying their debt, however, they spent the funds carousing and then moved on to the Dakota Territory.

Collins, the only one of the party who still had any money, built himself a fine house in Deadwood and furnished it properly. He sent for his mistress, Maude, whom he moved north from a brothel in Dallas, Texas. He bought a wagon and team and put Bass to work freighting between Cheyenne and Deadwood, but the venture did not pay. Soon the house became the headquarters for a group of desperadoes they called the Collins Gang, which consisted of Collins, Bass, and Davis who had come to Deadwood together. In addition they enlisted Jim Berry of Missouri; Bill Heffridge, alias Bill Cotts, of Pottsville, Pennsylvania; Tom Nixon; James F. "Frank" Towle; and Robert "Little Reddy" McKimie. The house became a notorious brothel, but even with the income from Maude's effort, there was not enough money to finance the wild lifestyles of eight men. They began to cast about for some new venture to supply their working capital.

The Black Hills Stage and Express line was carrying gold out of Deadwood and bringing in currency to finance the mining operations in Deadwood Gulch. On March 25, 1877, Collins, Bass, Towle, McKimie, Heffridge, and Berry tried to stop the down stagecoach when it was $2\frac{1}{2}$ miles south of town. When the coach came into view, McKimie opened fire with his shotgun loaded with heavy buckshot, killing driver Johnny Slaughter instantly, with fourteen lead pellets passing through his heart. A passenger who was riding next to the driver was wounded in his right arm by a stray pellet. The horses bolted at the sound of gunfire and ran half a mile, carrying the coach and passengers out of danger.

Persimmon Bill, an active road agent in the region, was at first suspected of the attempted highway robbery and murder, and this misdirection allowed the Collins Gang to make six more attacks on stagecoaches over the next few months. They tried on several occasions to stop the coaches by shooting the lead horses, the first pair in a team, but Collins and Bass made it clear that they would not condone the shooting of any person except in self defense. Following the first attempted robbery, McKimie was ejected from the gang and left Deadwood, as warned to do. Since none of the stagecoach robberies produced enough plunder to justify the risk or effort, Collins decided they needed a new line of work and began making plans to rob a train. As there were no trains in that part of the country, however, they stole a strong horse for each man and left, unsuspected and unmolested, for Nebraska.

Because Towle did not want to leave the Dakota Territory and had no interest in robbing trains, he quit the gang and joined up with "Big Nose" George Parrott and Charles Carey, stagecoach robbers. On September 13, 1878, road agents stopped a northbound stagecoach 4 miles south of Lance Creek and took the mail and express box before ordering the driver to continue on. When the southbound coach arrived at the same spot, one of the robbers stepped into the road, fired his gun, and ordered the driver to halt. Boone May and John Zimmerman were riding as messengers, and, when the shot was heard, May returned the gunfire with a shot of his own, killing the road agent. A gunfight then continued for thirty minutes, but the messengers could not dislodge the robbers, so the southbound coach continued on its way.

The following day a posse went to the scene, but the body of the dead road agent could not be found. Many doubted that May had killed his man until three months later when John Irwin, one of the robbers, was arrested and told where the body of Towle had been buried. May dug up the remains and cut off Towle's head, which he packed in a box. He carried his gruesome prize to Cheyenne, Laramie County, to collect the $200 reward, but the head was too decomposed to identify. He then took Towle's head to Carbon County, but he was also unable to collect the reward that had been posted there. He eventually disposed of the last of Frank Towle.

The six remaining members of the Collins Gang headed south with only $40 between them. They arrived near Ogallala, Nebraska, in early September and camped near the depot for a week while laying out a plan to rob a train. Collins developed his plan based upon his experiences with stagecoach robbery, finding a place where the train was stopped or could be stopped and easily boarded. Collins, who naturally took on the role of leader, chose to attack the Big Springs Station several miles west of town.

On the morning of September 19, 1877, six men rode freshly stolen horses to within one-half mile of the train station and hid their animals in the woods. A little after 10:00 P.M., the robbers rode to the station, captured agent George Barnhart and his assistant, and forced the agent to destroy his telegraph key. They left Berry and Nixon to guard them while they awaited the arrival of Union Pacific's eastbound train, No. 4 from San Francisco for Chicago, which was due at 10:48 P.M. When they heard the whistle in the distance, they took the agent out of the station and had him place a red warning lantern on the tracks, a sign of danger that no engineer could ignore, and the train stopped at the station platform. Collins and Heffridge, with cocked pistols, captured engineer George Vroman and the fireman, moved them into the station, and left them under the guard of Berry and Nixon. Collins and Heffridge then joined Bass and Davis in the express car.

Bass had already ordered express man Charles Miller, at gunpoint, to open the large iron safe, but Miller insisted that the safe was on a time lock and could not be opened until the clock ran down. After some discussion as to how they could coerce their captive to open the safe, he was pistol-whipped, but Miller produced a sheet of instructions explaining how the safe operated that proved that it could only be opened by combination after the time had elapsed.

Bass then took an ax and tried to chop his way into the safe, which contained $200,000 in gold but hardly scratched the surface. The men next rummaged through the car looking for treasure and found several large ingots of silver bullion, but these were too heavy to carry off without a strong wagon, which they lacked. Davis then found three wooden boxes sealed with wax that were addressed from the mint at San Francisco to a New York bank. Busting them open, he found $20,000 in newly minted gold coins in each box.

The men gathered up this plunder and $458 in currency before they went through the passengers, collecting $1,300 more in currency and four gold watches. When they heard the whistle of approaching freight train No. 10, they released the trainmen and allowed the Union

Pacific train to continue westbound. The robbers carried their plunder to their horses and fled, later dividing it into piles of 500 coins each and placing each share in a sturdy sack.

Tom Nixon and Jim Berry then started out together, but Nixon soon left Berry, saying he was going on to Florida, though in fact turned north into Canada and was not heard of again. Nixon had covered his trail so well that thirty years later the Pinkertons still believed he had fled to the British Honduras and used his share of the loot to start a business. Berry returned to his home in Mexico, Missouri. He spent lavishly, raising some suspicion because all the coins he presented had been struck in 1877. Noticing the suspicion as he spent his loot, he tried to exchange his remaining $9,000 for currency, taking $3,000 in coins to each of three banks, believing this would disguise his purpose. However, he was already being watched, and the law was soon on his trail. The officers went to his house to arrest him but found him sleeping outside, not far from his home, as a precaution against being captured. They surrounded the fugitive and ordered his surrender, but Berry drew his gun to make a fight of it. He was wounded in the right leg, disarmed, arrested, taken into town, and lodged in jail. The wound did not seem serious at first, and he was expected to recover, but soon infection set in and Berry died of gangrene poisoning in two days.

Collins and Heffridge started out together and on September 23, four days after the robbery, were seen crossing the Republican River in Nebraska, making their way toward Kansas. Sheriff George W. Bardsley of Ellis County, Kansas, believed that the robbers would head in his direction so he started toward Hays City with a posse of ten U.S. Cavalry troopers and a detective. He stopped at Buffalo Station 60 miles from Hays City, a desolate area where travelers were almost sure to pass, and set up a camp in a ravine, out of sight from the station, to watch for the fugitives. Three days after the robbers were seen in Nebraska, two men leading a pack pony rode up to the station and stopped. The sheriff was looking for a party of six men so he dismissed the pair as innocent travelers. Collins went to Thompson's Store and made some purchases but, while searching through his pockets for money, exposed a letter that was addressed to Joel Collins. The sheriff was informed.

Collins had no way of knowing that he had been identified by Andrew Riley, one of the passengers on the train who had known him in Deadwood, so he made no effort to hide his identity when the sheriff joined him for several drinks later. Collins and Heffridge were allowed to leave town, for the safety of the residents, but the posse soon overtook them on the trail. When Sheriff Bardsley asked them to return to town to further investigate the matter, they agreed, insisting that they were just two cattle buyers from Texas returning home. However, after riding several hundred yards, both men decided to make their fight and drew their pistols. Before they could fire a single shot, both train robbers were riddled with bullets and killed instantly.

Bass and Davis went south into Texas but bypassed Denton and went directly through to Fort Worth. After staying there several days, Davis decided to continue on to New Orleans, Louisiana, while Bass went on to Cooke County. Bass set up a camp in Cave Hollow, a narrow ravine choked by brush and honeycombed with caves, and began recruiting men he could trust as part of the Bass Gang. His first recruits were Frank Jackson and Henry Underwood. The three would-be robbers traveled to San Antonio and went on a spree. Although they seemed unaware that two lawmen were in town watching them, they suddenly packed their kits and disappeared. They returned to Cave Hollow where Bass still had a substantial number of $20 gold coins buried, but it was decided that the operations of the Bass Gang should be financed by funds mutually obtained from some robbery. Or perhaps Bass simply wanted to test his new partners in crime. Bass fell back on a plan with which he felt more comfortable—robbing stage-coaches. On December 22, 1877, three masked road agents stopped a coach near Fort Worth. They did not molest the mails and there was no treasure box, but the two passengers contributed a measly $11. The boys returned to their hideout, and Underwood went on to spend Christmas with his family.

On the night of December 24, 1877, Underwood's house was surrounded by lawmen, and he was mistakenly arrested as the train robber Tom Nixon. Underwood was taken to Kearney, Nebraska, and lodged in jail to await trial for the Big Springs train robbery. The authorities were so sure they had the right man that they paid out the $500 reward. Although Underwood could have easily proved an alibi through the testimony of a number of reputable witnesses, he reckoned these men would be Texans testifying in Nebraska and so decided that he could not take the chance and must take the matter into his own hands.

In jail he met "Arkansas" Johnson, whose real name was Huckston. Johnson's wife smuggled in several saw blades in the false bottom of a bucket; Underwood made another saw out of the shank taken from the sole of an old discarded boot; and they managed to obtain a vial of nitric acid. They used the nitric acid to soften the metal of the bars so they could saw through and then, using the metal dust mixed with soap to make a paste, filled the gaps to disguise their work. It took the two men three weeks to cut through, and they made their escape on March 14, 1878. They nearly froze and starved to death while heading south, but after seventeen days reached Denton, Texas, where both men joined the Bass Gang.

CHAPTER THREE

SAM BASS, TERROR OF THE TEXAS TRAINS

Although Sam Bass had led Joel Collins into a life of crime, in the Dakota Territory, Collins, applying his natural business acumen, had naturally evolved into the leader of the gang, and Bass had become the pupil. When Bass returned to Texas, he was intent on making the most of all he had learned from Collins, so he began forming the Bass Gang, which would eventually go on a spree launched by the first successful robbery of a train in Texas. It took considerable effort, but he finally managed to recruit Frank Jackson. Along with Henry Underwood, they went to San Antonio for several weeks. On December 22, 1877, all three men stopped the eastbound stagecoach between Cleburne and Fort Worth. They got only $11 from the two passengers, missing several hundreds that were hidden. After Underwood was arrested on Christmas Eve, Bass and Jackson laid low in Cave Hollow hidden among the heavy brush and caves. Bass was not, however, content with the quiet life, and both men were still committed to financing gang operations with mutually acquired funds. By mid-January Bass was hard at work planning their next robbery.

On January 26, 1878, Bass and Jackson, carefully disguised by masks, stopped the coach between Weatherford and Forth Worth at

Mary's Creek. As the stage was ascending a steep bank and had to slow, the two road agents ordered the driver to halt. Once again they ignored the mails and found that there was no express box, but they collected $70 from the five passengers, though some reports suggest the loot totaled nearly $500 and three watches. Since this was the ninth stage-coach robbed by Bass—seven near Deadwood and two near Fort Worth—and none had carried the payoff he had anticipated, he once again concluded that his fortune would be found aboard railroad express cars. He began making his plan to rob a train using Collins's method, which applied the *modus operandi* for robbing stagecoaches—choosing a place where the train was stopped or could be stopped and easily boarded. He was sure that two men could not pull off the robbery as he had planned it so he recruited Seaborn Barnes of Tarrant County and Tom Spotswood from Little Elm Creek in Denton County.

On Thursday night of February 21, 1878, the four aspiring train robbers rode to Allen Station, which was located 24 miles north of Dallas in Collin County, or about 6 miles north of McKinney. The following night they donned masks and captured the station agent. The south-bound Houston & Texas Central (H&TC) No. 4 train arrived in a few minutes and made its scheduled stop. The H&TC Railway had gotten its charter on March 11, 1848, but by 1861 had only 81 miles of track opened when the Civil War interrupted track laying. The gauge of the tracks laid was 5 feet 6 inches; but when the standard 4-feet-8½-inch gauge was adopted by Texas in 1875, the rail lines were converted to this standard. The railway instituted Pullman service in 1872 so that the train, as it arrived at Allen Station on that fateful night, was represented by all the modern conveniences offered by trains in the West, including three sleepers, a passenger car, a baggage car, and an express car.

Engineer William Sullivan and his fireman were captured at gun-point and marched in front as a shield in approaching the express car. Bass sent Barnes running through the passenger cars announcing that "fifty to sixty heavily armed desperadoes" were robbing the train, thus discouraging the passengers from interfering. When the three robbers and two train men reached the express car, they found the door shut and locked and express agent James Thomas refusing to yield. However, after shots were exchanged and Thomas was out of ammunition, he opened the door and admitted Bass and Spotswood, while Jackson stood guard over the engineer and fireman. Though the masks fully disguised the robbers' faces, Thomas noted, as the men searched through the packages, that one of the robbers had a peculiar glass eye. Bass and Spotswood reportedly found about $3,000 among the car's contents, though Bass would later state that they had divided only $1,280. They then sent the train on its way. The robbers fled into Denton County, and from there Spotswood, leaving behind his share of the plunder with Bass, returned to his ranch on Little Elm Creek.

The people were outraged by this, the first successful robbery of a train in Texas. The governor, the railroad, and the express company immediately posted rewards. Four days after the robbery, a posse led by W. L. Cornish captured Spotswood based upon the description of his peculiar glass eye. The rancher denied any part in the robbery but was tried in late June and convicted on July 2. He was sentenced to serve ten years in prison but was granted a motion for a new trial based upon additional evidence. After his attorneys obtained a continuance to the spring term of the Collin County District Court and, through this delay and other manipulations of the law, allowed the public's anger to cool, Spotswood was acquitted of the charge at his second trial. He never weakened and refused to "peach" on his fellow train robbers.

The take at Allen Station confirmed Bass's belief that his fortune was being carried by the railroads; while Spotswood was in jail, Bass was planning another train robbery. This time he chose Hutchins, a small way station 10 miles south of Dallas consisting of only twenty-five buildings. Shortly before 10:00 P.M. on March 18, Bass, Jackson, and Barnes rode to the station and captured the agent and his assistant. The southbound H&TC train arrived on schedule a few minutes later and, as the train slowed to a stop, Jackson jumped aboard the engine and captured the engineer and fireman while Bass and Barnes captured two stowaway tramps riding on the "blind baggage." They used their four prisoners as a shield to approach the express car.

Warned by mail clerk R. Terrell that a robbery was in progress, express agent Henry "Heck" Thomas, brother of agent James Thomas, barred the door, hid inside the pot-bellied stove all the treasure he could immediately locate, and took his position behind a barricade with six-shooter in hand. Shots were exchanged, but Thomas, in his haste to hide the treasure, had forgotten to secure his extra cartridges; when his pistol was empty, he had to surrender. Two robbers entered the express car and went through the mails and other packages but found only $500 before sending the train on its way. Henry Thomas was later hailed as a hero and rewarded for saving nearly all of the treasure in the care of his company.

The robbers fled toward the Trinity River bottom as the station agent telegraphed their description throughout the region, and posses were soon in the field. However, the trail of the three robbers was soon lost. The Bass Gang was now wanted for a federal offense as well, but as soon as they were settled in their hideout, Bass began planning a third train robbery. Barnes had taken ill and was too sick to participate, so Bass and Jackson rode to Eagle Ford Station, 6 miles west of Dallas, to look over the situation. Although they agreed it would be the next place for a robbery, they could not proceed with only two men, so they waited.

During the lull Frank Jackson, upon the urging of his family, withdrew from the gang, leaving Bass alone with an ailing Barnes. On March 31, Henry Underwood and "Arkansas" Johnson arrived from Nebraska and joined Bass in Cave Hollow. When Underwood declined to participate in the Eagle Ford robbery because he wanted to spend time with his family after his long absence, Bass and Johnson recruited two novices who were never identified. The four robbers rode to Eagle Ford Station where they hid beneath the platform late on the evening of April 4 to await the westbound Texas & Pacific express train.

The Texas & Pacific Railway Company was the only railroad in the state operating under a federal charter, which had been granted by Congress on March 3, 1871, although it had received its state charter on

February 16, 1852. It was originally planned as part of a southern transcontinental railway, but the plan never materialized. The line from Eagle Ford to Fort Worth was completed in July 1876, and by 1881 the T&PR was operating on 972 miles of track, all within Texas.

Just before 11:00 P.M. Bass captured station agent E. L Stevens. As soon as the eastbound train stopped, Bass and Johnson boarded the engine and captured the engineer and his fireman. They added the agent, several more trainmen, and a passenger to the prisoners and then ordered the agent to approach the express car and request entrance. They found that express man J. H. Hickox and messenger Clarence E. Groce had bolted the door and refused to open it. After Bass beat on the door with a heavy stick and gave them two minutes to open up, Hickox unlocked the door. The robbers found only $50 in the express car, so they went through the mail car and took twenty-seven registered letters containing $234. Surprisingly, there was no resistance even though the express agent and guard were well armed. After the robbery the two novices returned home with their small share of the plunder, thoroughly cured of their adventurous spirit, while Bass and Johnson vacationed in Dallas County for several days.

Once Bass was again safe in Cave Hollow, he began planning another train robbery and chose Mesquite Station 12 miles east of Dallas. For this robbery he would take along six men, including Johnson; Underwood, who was now ready to participate; Jackson, who had returned to the gang; William Collins, who was a brother of Joel Collins; and novices Albert Herndon and Sam Pipes of Dallas County, who had enlisted after the Eagle Ford robbery.

On April 10, 1878, the Bass Gang rode to Mesquite Station and, leaving Collins to hold their horses, captured station agent Jake Zurn. Mesquite at that time consisted of a general store, blacksmith shop, two saloons, and several houses, so the robbers were aware they could face some resistance from the townsfolk.

When the westbound Texas & Pacific No. 1 train arrived at 11:00 P.M., Jackson jumped aboard the engine and captured engineer J. Barron, but fireman Tom Mooney, upon seeing a masked man with a cocked

Sam Bass in his youth
WESTERN HISTORY COLLECTIONS, UNIVERSITY OF OKLAHOMA LIBRARIES

revolver, jumped off and hid under the platform. Express man Spofford Kerley, mail clerk William Towers, and guards J. Allen and J. G. Lynch were warned by baggage master Ben Caperton that the train was being robbed. Kerley saw the robbers and fired several shots before bolting his door, but all his shots missed their target. Conductor Julius "Jules"

Alvord heard the commotion and joined in the affray. As he had only a two-shot derringer in his vest pocket, however, he went in search of a six-shooter after firing both barrels.

Meanwhile a convict train, stopped on a siding, was staffed with a full complement of armed guards who opened fire on the robbers from the car but could not leave their prisoners to get closer. When they ran low on ammunition, they ceased firing for fear they would run out and be overpowered by the convicts. However, while this firefight was in progress, baggage master Caperton opened his door and fired both barrels of his shotgun at the robbers. A few moments later, a candy vendor in the passenger cars opened fire with his tiny revolver. Through all this gunfire, Jackson was slightly wounded in both legs and Pipes received a slight wound in his side. Conductor Alvord returned with a six-shooter, but before he could inflict any wounds, he was shot in the left wrist. The bullet traveled up the arm and exited at the elbow, shattering the arm bone and completely disabling him.

The gang was about to abandon the robbery when the shooting ceased, so they doused the express car with coal oil and threatened to burn it. The men in the express car discussed their options and surrendered, but not before Kerley hid all the treasure in his charge except for $200. The robbers entered but, now fearing a force of men from the tiny village, decided not to search and took this small amount before they hurriedly rode off.

Posses were soon in the field. Over the next two months, some posse was always on the trail or awaiting word of a sighting so it could respond. There were several confrontations during this time, but in the running gun battles only two lawmen were slightly wounded and two horses killed. Finally, on June 13, 1878, a posse burst in upon the camp of the Bass Gang on Salt Creek near Cottondale in Wise County, and Johnson was killed instantly by a bullet through his brain. Underwood was seriously wounded but managed to escape. Having had enough of this game, he took his family and fled to Indiana. He settled there and spent a large part of the remainder of his life in Indiana's prisons.

Pipes and Herndon were soon arrested for their part in the Mesquite robbery, the only members of the Bass Gang to be tried and convicted of train robbery. They were sent to prison for ninety-nine years, but both men were pardoned in 1886. Herndon then disappeared and was not heard of again. Pipes, though he remained a law-abiding citizen, was once again mentioned in the newspapers when he accidentally shot himself to death several years after gaining his freedom.

Bill Collins fled to Pembria on the Canadian border but was finally tracked down by deputy U.S. Marshal Bill Anderson. When the plucky lawman tried to arrest the fugitive single-handedly in a store, they exchanged shots, both men dying from their wounds. Bill's brother, Henry, was tracked to Grayson County where he too was shot to death while resisting arrest. Jim Murphy and his father, who had harbored and supplied the fugitives, were arrested as accessories to the robberies, but Jim Murphy, concerned for his father's health, made a deal to have the charges dropped in return for aiding in the capture of Bass. He joined Bass, Jackson, and Barnes as they traveled around the country avoiding posses and searching for one last big haul to finance their escape from Texas. Murphy talked them out of robbing banks in Waco and Belton, as he had not been able to alert the lawmen, while all the time steering them toward Round Rock where he hoped the band could be taken alive. The four men arrived at Round Rock on July 19, 1878, and Murphy made some excuse to stop at a store at one end of town while the other men went further on toward another store located across from the bank.

Bass, Jackson, and Barnes rode to the back of an alley across from Koppel's General Store, and Jackson stayed with the horses. Barnes and Bass crossed the street to make several purchases and look over the bank, which they planned to rob the following day. Two deputy sheriffs, who were under orders from the county sheriff to have the arms of all strangers checked in at their office, saw that the men were armed. Deputy A. W. Grimes, with deputy Moore outside, approached Bass and Barnes in the store and asked about their revolvers, but before any conversation could begin, both fugitives drew their pistols and began firing at the deputy. Grimes turned and ran but was shot five times in the back and died instantly, his six-shooter still in his holster. His partner, deputy Moore, was also wounded and unable to do more than wound Bass's hand before he collapsed.

Lawmen, positioned at various places throughout the town, responded to the sound of the shooting and took up the fight. Bass and Barnes returned fire and managed to reach their horses, but as soon as Barnes was in his saddle, ranger Dick Ware, taking deliberate aim, shot him through the head, killing him instantly. George Herold then called for Bass and Jackson to surrender, but the gang's leader turned and clicked an empty pistol at the lawman, which he had been unable to reload with his wounded hand. Herold returned fire, and the ball struck Bass in the back, while he was trying to control his cantankerous horse, and exited by his navel. Jackson then dismounted, helped Bass mount, remounted his own horse, and, taking the reins, led his leader out of town on the run.

A posse was soon on the trail of the two fugitives but was unable to continue the pursuit after dark. The posse resumed its search the following morning and found Bass, weak from loss of blood, propped against a tree not far from a railroad construction camp. Jackson had tried to dress the wound and carry his friend to safety, but Bass could not continue and ordered his friend to go on without him. Jackson, seeing the futility of taking Bass any further without a doctor's care, finally agreed to leave and was not heard of again for twenty years. In 1899 Jackson, under the alias William F. "Bill" Downing, resurfaced at Willcox, Arizona, and once again was involved in several train robberies.

Bass was taken to Round Rock where doctors examined him and pronounced his wound fatal. Several times he was encouraged to make an ante-mortem statement, to bare his soul before he died, but he would not "peach" on any living member of his gang or any supporter. He surprised everyone when he seemed to rally on Sunday morning, July 21, but after noon his condition began to deteriorate rapidly. He died on his twenty-sixth birthday a few minutes after 3:30 P.M.

CHAPTER FOUR

WRECKED AND BUNGLED AT CAPE HORN

By 1881 Northern California had been a hotbed of criminal activity for a quarter century while Southern California, though it had its share of miscreants, had been spared the worst of the criminal epidemic. Most of the mineral wealth of California was in the north, and this drew the worst of the hard cases there to ply their trade. There were, of course, highwaymen active in the south, but their activities were rare in comparison to the gangs and lone road agents operating in the north. Road agents preyed upon travelers, freighters, and stagecoaches, but train robbery was unheard of west of the Sierra Nevadas. The first train robbery in the West had occurred at Verdi, Nevada, in 1871, east of the mountain range, and within a few hours the same train was robbed at Pequop, Nevada. It was just a matter of time before criminals in Southern California would try for the big haul, and they would have to assault a train to capture it.

Ed Steinigal was a gold miner determined to find his fortune, and if he could not find mineral wealth in the ground, then he would take it from others who had been successful. He fell in with George H. Shinn, a gambler who was known to cheat at cards and frequent brothels. In late summer 1881 the two men enlisted the help of three more men, as the work they planned could not be done by just two. The first man they involved was Ruben Rogers, a gold miner who lived at Pickering Bar on the north fork of the American River, because his cabin was near the tracks of the Southern Pacific Railroad. From the Rogers cabin there was a trail to the Cape Horn Mills about 5 miles from Colfax, near the tracks of the Central Pacific Railroad. Henry Frazier, the second recruit, was also a gold miner and well acquainted with the explosives used by miners, Hercules giant powder cartridges. The third recruit was John Mason, a teamster working at Iowa Hill. They told the three new recruits that they had a scheme that would make them all rich, and the men, who had not become wealthy in their legitimate lines of work, were interested.

On August 30, 1881, Steinigal, Shinn, and Mason met Frazier at Rogers's cabin at 2:00 P.M. where the two leaders laid out their plans. Steinigal had a gun on his shoulder and another in a sack, and the two men told the new men that they had hidden some tools nearby in the brush. They had stocked the cabin with four days' provisions, which they had taken from the Aurora blacksmith shop. When the tools were retrieved, the two leaders displayed two picks, two shovels, several axes, a wrench, a hatchet, a sledge hammer, two pairs of boots, eight pounds of nails, and giant powder cartridges, fuse, and caps. It was decided that after dark on the following night, the men would take all the tools to the tracks at Cape Horn and remove a rail.

On the night of August 31, Steinigal, Shinn, and Mason showed at the cabin, but Rogers and Frazier were not there, so the men went to the spring near the railway cut and sat down near the tracks to wait. Rogers appeared at 9:00 P.M. with a shotgun and a six-shooter, the sack containing twenty-four cartridges of giant powder, fuse and caps, a wrench, and several bottles of whiskey to fortify their resolve. He carried a lantern, but it was not yet lit. When Rogers got to the spring, all the men had a drink of water and some whiskey. Rogers laid down his monkey wrench, which he forgot to retrieve before they left.

Steinigal, Shinn, Rogers, and Mason went down to the tracks and met Frazier on the way. Frazier was to make an iron bar to pry up the rail

Ed Steinigal
WELLS FARGO BANK, N.A.

and, if he had not, then the affair would have to be postponed. But Frazier had made the bar, so the party of five went into the bushes and loaded two guns, then went to the tracks, which were on a grade. They used the bar to take up the right-hand rail and pulled the higher point out. They pressed the lower part of the rail into the dirt, thinking this would disguise it so the engineer could not see it was tampered with. It was a difficult task removing the rail, and the bar broke once during the operation, but finally the rail was loosened by Mason and Shinn, while Steinigal and Rogers went on the tracks as lookouts. The men went to a place near the telegraph poles and put on their masks, then took several large drinks of whiskey and smashed the bottles. They hunkered down to await the arrival of the train.

The eastbound Central Pacific No. 1 train, pulled by two engines, came slowly up the grade at 11:47 P.M. As it came around a gentle curve, both locomotives were thrown off the tracks, followed by the tender, a fruit car, and the express and baggage coaches. Once the train came to a halt, fireman Fred Boyd jumped free, but was immediately captured by one of the robbers holding a shotgun. The robber threatened to blow his head off if he moved, but Boyd ignored the threat and fled along the side of the train. Meanwhile, one of the passengers went through the cars, calming the excited passengers. The Wells, Fargo & Co. messenger, N. M. Chadwick, slid open his door to see what had happened and was met by John Mason, who pointed his gun at Chadwick and yelled, "You s__ of a b___, fall out of there!"

Chadwick slammed and locked the door, extinguished the lantern, drew his six-shooter, and prepared for the fight he was sure would soon follow. However, the five robbers turned their attention to the mail car and confronted U.S. mail agent Louis Tripp with their firearms and ordered him to raise his hands. Tripp also ignored the robbers and refused to move. By then curious passengers were starting to disembark to see what had happened to their train.

One of the robbers called out, "This is a freight train!" Just then Mason noticed that Shinn and Frazier were standing motionless looking

George H. Shinn
WELLS FARGO BANK, N.A.

down the tracks, and he yelled for them to get busy with the work. Frazier replied that he saw soldiers coming off the train, thinking the large number of passengers were soldiers, and Steinigal yelled, "It's too big to take!"

Mason replied, "Well, if we are going, we had better go quick."

At that the five men ran into the brush. They left behind their tools and a note that read, "Sacramento, May 20. Dick, will be at Stump's Ret's, Ne City, Monday. Everything O.K. 349."

After they had run some distance, Frazier said, "We have done enough now. We better go home," and they separated. Rogers went to his home in Gold Run while the rest went to Rogers's cabin.

As soon as the robbers had fled, conductor Charles Allen walked back to Colfax and telegraphed Auburn and Sacramento. A special train was dispatched to bring in the passengers and baggage, and a crew was sent to put the train back on the tracks. It took eight hours to get the No. 1 under way again.

At dawn Sheriff John Boggs took his posse to the scene and launched his investigation. They began to inventory all the equipment they found, including twenty-four Hercules giant powder cartridges and fuses, all the tools, masks, and the note. Boggs knew that Stump's Restaurant in Nevada City was a hangout for every sort of criminal type and thought that the robbery might have been planned and staged from there. Rewards of $2,000 were offered, and the detectives of each concerned company were rushed to the scene by special train, including James Hume and John Thacker from Wells, Fargo & Company; Fred Burke, Len Harris, and Bill Hickey from the railroad; and San Francisco Police Department's Captain A. W. Stone. They began running down every clue and sighting, and soon learned that the note was a plant to steer them in the wrong direction. They made a few arrests, but the men were proved innocent of this crime and released.

Certain that the robbers were local miners, Boggs made inquiries. He learned that Ed Steinigal had recently purchased a large number of Hercules giant powder cartridges and fuse, so, with Jim Hume, he rode to the cabin at Pickering Bar on September 9. When he found Mason and Steinigal there, they insisted that they were miners even though they had no tools. The lawmen searched the cabin and found material that matched the masks found by the tracks. They next found shovels and picks, with the handles cut off, sunk in the river. The men were closely questioned, but Steinigal was firm. Mason, however, was convinced that he could only save his neck if he "peached" on his fellow robbers, and Boggs convinced him that they had a good case against them, so he confessed and named the other four men. He would later draw a map showing every movement of the men at the tracks.

The lawmen began searching for the robbers and arrested Henry Frazier the following day. They learned from Frazier that Rogers had just eloped with Mary Sullivan from Iowa Hill. They tracked them to the Union Hotel in Nevada City where the newlywed couple was spending their honeymoon night, and Hume sent a telegram to City Marshal Erastus Baldridge asking him to arrest Rogers. Baldridge arrested Rogers at daybreak when the couple came down to breakfast.

All four of the robbers under arrest were brought into Auburn and lodged in the county jail, but Mason was soon moved to Sacramento to protect him from the other prisoners. The search for Shinn continued until October 27, when Fred Burke, the railroad detective who played such a major role in the arrest of the Verdi train robbers, captured Shinn when the fugitive stopped at the Doolin Ranch in Antelope Valley, 18 miles west of Maxwell in Colusa County. Shinn was taken back to Auburn and lodged in jail with the other three robbers. The four prisoners hired several of the best attorneys in California, so Wells, Fargo & Co. and the Central Pacific Railroad hired two special prosecutors to assist District Attorney Bill Lardner. This strategy would backfire on the prosecution as the trial was costing the citizens a great deal of their tax dollars and, conveniently, the public learned that the railroad had refused to pay its taxes for several years and was $90,000 in arrears. This gave the appearance that the railroad wanted the people to subsidize their trials.

Steinigal's trial began on November 11, 1881, and took twenty-one days because each side called fifty witnesses and the number of prosecution witnesses gave credence to the belief that the defendants were being persecuted by the railroad. One of the strongest pieces of evidence was the note, which matched the handwriting of letters sent from the jail by Steinigal and intercepted by deputies. There was no analysis of the handwriting permitted by the court, but a simple comparison of the handwriting by jurors was allowed, as it was believed that each man's handwriting was unique. Even though the jury saw clearly that it was Steinigal's handwriting, still it could not bring in a verdict, so Steinigal was retried three months later. This time he was convicted of attempted robbery and sentenced to serve thirteen years at San Quentin Prison.

The case of Shinn, the next to be tried, began on June 26, 1882. Now the public concern for the cost had escalated, fueled by newspaper reports, but Shinn was also convicted. On July 18 he was sentenced to serve twelve years and eight months at the San Quentin Prison. Mason had testified against each man and had remained free in consideration of turning state's evidence. On September 11, 1882, Rogers and Frazier's trial began. By then both Steinigal and Shinn were at the prison and had confessed, corroborating Mason's story.

Steinigal agreed to return to Auburn and repeat his confession on the stand, which the prosecution decided would strengthen the testimony of Mason. With the trial already under way, Sheriff Boggs went to the San Quentin Prison and took Steinigal back to Auburn.

On September 13 Boggs was met at the depot by his twenty-one-year-old son, John, when the train arrived at 10:00 P.M. The train had been filled with passengers returning home from the state fair, and as they disembarked, the streets quickly became crowded. Steinigal was handcuffed, but his ankles were not shackled as he had to walk from the train to the courthouse where the jail was located. When they neared their destination, the prisoner saw his opportunity and jumped in front of two girls, ran quickly into a dark alley, and disappeared. Both lawmen drew their pistols but could not fire for fear of hitting an innocent bystander. The lawmen called for everyone to get down. Once their field of fire was cleared, they each fired several rounds but without effect, and Steinigal escaped.

The following morning a posse, led by Boggs, followed the trail to a creek bed 6 miles north of town where they found the handcuffs, which Steinigal had managed to break off. They lost the trail there, and the fugitive was never recaptured, even though the state offered a reward of $300. Now with only Mason to testify against Frazier and Rogers and the ill feelings toward the railroad and their prosecutors, some of the jurors accepted the alibi of Rogers and could not arrive at a verdict. The two defendants were retried in December, and two days before Christmas the jury returned a unanimous verdict acquitting both men.

Since Mason was freed in consideration of his turning state's evidence, Steinigal had escaped and was never heard of again, and Rogers and Frazier were acquitted, Shinn was the only train wrecker still in prison. He served his time as a model prisoner and earned a position as an outside trusty. Because he was allowed to leave the prison unsupervised, there was little concern when, on a rainy December 1, 1887, he drove a horse-drawn cart out of the front gates. Unknown to the guards who remained indoors, he had Charles Dorsey hidden in the cart and both men escaped.

They remained at large until 1890 when someone notified authorities where they could be found. Wells, Fargo & Company sent Hume to Chicago where, with a force of men from the Pinkerton Detective Agency, he arrested the two fugitives. Hume learned that the two men had been traveling west periodically to commit all sorts of crimes, including stagecoach holdups. Shinn was returned to California in late October 1890 but was sent to Folsom to separate him from his partner in the escape, who returned to San Quentin. They were never prosecuted for the rash of crimes committed while they were fugitives. Shinn spent another nine years in prison on his original charge and was released in 1899. He then disappeared from the criminal records of California.

CHAPTER FIVE

THE KIT JOY GANG

On November 24, 1883, the eastbound Southern Pacific No. 19 train coming from San Francisco to Deming, New Mexico, was 4 miles west of Gage Station and 15 miles from Deming when fireman Thomas North yelled out, "My God. There's a hole in the track!"

Engineer Theophelus C. Webster set the brakes but it was too late. The engine, tender, and first three cars were derailed. The two trainmen rode the engine until it stopped and then, fearing the boiler would explode, the fireman jumped off with Webster close behind. When Webster appeared at the door of the engine cab he was shot twice, one bullet piercing his heart and killing him instantly. The engineer fell near the tracks right beside his ditched engine.

Conductor T. Zach Vail and a passenger named Gaskell went forward to investigate and see what help they could provide. The two men were met by four unmasked, armed men who robbed Vail of his gold watch and $200 he had collected from late-boarding passengers. From Gaskell, a Chicago publisher, they took $155 but returned his watch when he said it had sentimental value. It was 4:20 P.M., so the robbers, four in number, were in no rush as they seemed to be waiting on darkness to make their escape. When the robbers battered in the door of the express car, the stunned messenger put up no resistance as they took their time going through the car, where they found $1,800 in the safe. They next went to the mail car but could find nothing of value.

By the time they had finished their work, the sun had set, so they loaded their plunder, mounted their horses, and fled north toward Grant County. Brakeman Tom Scott was sent to Gage Station on foot where he tried to telegraph to Deming for help, but the lines had been cut, so he telegraphed to San Francisco, then through Denver to Deming. By 10:00 P.M. a special train was en route to the scene to transfer the passengers and baggage. In the morning Deputy Dan Tucker, with fifty armed men including several excellent trackers, took up the trail. However, after traveling a half dozen miles, the trail led onto hard, rocky ground where all sign was lost, so the posse gave up the chase. A company of soldiers from Fort Huachuca also took the field but had no better luck. There were no clues and even the reward of over $2,500 produced no leads. The lawmen had no choice but to wait patiently for a break in the case.

A month after the robbery, Albert C. Eaton, the owner of a hay camp 9 miles from Gage Station, contacted Harvey Whitehill, sheriff of Grant County, and said that on November 23 four indigent cowboys named Joy, Taggart, Lee, and Cleveland had stopped at his camp. From their peculiar behavior he suspected they were up to something but mistakenly thought they were rustling stock in the area. When he questioned them, they were evasive in their answers, so he made a point of carefully examining their animals, which consisted of three horses and a mule ridden by Cleveland, for later identification. When he found that there was no rustling going on at that time and then heard of the train robbery, he suspected the four cowboys.

Whitehill followed up on the lead himself and made several discreet inquiries, from which he learned that on the day following the robbery, Taggart, Lee, and Cleveland had been seen in Silver City, all supposed to be out-of-work cowboys but no longer looking for work. Whitehill knew by sight all four men named by Eaton, especially Joy, who had once been an employee on the sheriff's ranch. In addition, the four

Sheriff Harvey Whitehill
THE SILVER CITY MUSEUM

men had visited his ranch on November 29. The descriptions were distributed throughout the territory. Cleveland was described as "a large ugly Negro, about 6 feet in height, as black as Erebus, and has been in this neighborhood for nearly two years." Mitch Lee was described as "a native Texan, 21 years of age, 5 feet 8 inches tall with black hair and brown eyes, and dark complected." Frank Taggart was "twenty-six years old, 5 feet 8 inches tall, with light-colored hair, blue eyes, and a fair complexion, and had dark tobacco stains about his mouth and teeth which

John W. Gilmo
YUMA TERRITORIAL PRISON STATE PARK

were plainly seen when he smiled, which was often." The leader of the gang, Kit Joy, had been born in Burnet County, Texas, in 1869 and was described as "missing several front teeth, nearly blind in his right eye, 5 feet 10 inches tall and weight 140 pounds; light complected with blue eyes and brown hair."

Whitehill told what he had learned to Wells, Fargo & Company's lead detective, James Hume, who had been following up every lead after his arrival in New Mexico with fellow detective J. N. Thacker. Hume soon learned that Joy, Lee, and Taggart had been loitering about the Duck Creek country before the train wrecking but had disappeared, with Cleveland, just afterwards. They found one of the camps and there retrieved a copy of the Placer, California, *Herald* newspaper, which they traced to a saloon in Silver City. The owner remembered the four cowboys being there and making several small purchases, and it was supposed they had taken his copy of the *Herald*. Hume sent out inquiries and learned that Cleveland had been seen in Socorro. Whitehill went to Socorro and contacted County Sheriff Pedro S. Simpson, who agreed to help.

On December 28 Whitehill, a large powerful man, approached Cleveland in the lobby of a hotel and offered his right hand in greeting. Cleveland took it and the sheriff tightened his grip and would not let go until Sheriff Simpson got the drop on Cleveland and they arrested him. They questioned Cleveland, but their prisoner would admit to nothing. They were certain he would not "peach" on his fellow robbers, so Whitehill told him that the others were in jail and had confessed. Whitehill told Cleveland that all the other robbers had identified him as the man who shot Webster, and this upset Cleveland so thoroughly that he confessed and confirmed the names of the three men who had robbed the train with him, insisting that it was Lee who had shot Webster. Cleveland gave such a detailed confession of the robbery that there was no doubt of its truth, so he was taken back to Grant County, jailed, and then learned how he had been fooled by Whitehill.

Word was spread naming and describing the wanted men, and Deputy Sheriff John W. Gilmo learned that Frank Taggart was in La Parte el Frio in Socorro County. On January 6, 1884, Gilmo, with a Mexican guide and a small posse, found Taggart rounding up 200 head of cattle he had just purchased, presumably with the stolen money. They arrested him, saying it was only for horse stealing to avoid a fight, and Taggart soon joined Cleveland in the Silver City jail.

Near the end of January, Joy and Lee went to the ranch of the Lyons & Campbell Cattle Company looking for work. The boys had stopped at Horse Springs and were seen by Deputy Sheriff Andrew J. Best and Charles C. Perry. They fit the description of the two train robbers still on the run, so after they left the springs, Best and Perry caught them on the trail and proposed that they join them in a raid on the Soccoro County jail to free murderer Joel Fowler. The two lawmen said Joy and Lee would be well paid for doing their part in the jail delivery, so the two fugitives agreed to help spring Fowler and returned to Horse Springs. As soon as Joy and Lee had fallen asleep, they were disarmed and captured. They were turned over to Socorro County Sheriff Simpson who took them to Silver City and lodged them in jail with Taggart and Cleveland.

Sheriff Whitehill had been dismissed soon after Taggart was captured, under charges that he had neglected his duties while chasing the train robbers. He was replaced by George M. Smith. Smith's jail policy was that each day the prisoners, four at a time, were given fifteen minutes in the yard for exercise and fresh air. On March 10, 1884, jailer Steve Wilson and one other guard were watching four men in the yard. When their exercise time was up, he started them for their cells, but the prisoners suddenly turned on the two lawmen and overpowered them. The two officers said later that the struggle lasted for a full ten minutes, but their calls for help went unheeded, so the prisoners finally took their weapons and locked them in a cell. They opened the other cells and invited all the prisoners to join them, but only convicted murderer Carlos Chavez and horse thief Charles Spencer came out. They captured the Chinese cook and locked him in there so he could not sound the alarm.

The escapees went through the guardroom, captured guard Nick Ware, who was asleep, and put him in the cell with the others. They then went into the armory and took six-shooters, one shotgun, and one Winchester rifle, all that was there. They also found a hammer and cold chisel and removed their shackles, leaving them on the floor of the guardroom before they slipped out of the jail. As they went through the front office, they were discovered by Deputy Sheriff Tom Hall who, unarmed, slammed the door to the rear rooms, locked it behind him, and went for his guns. He sounded the alarm as the prisoners fled down Market Street, going directly to the Elephant Corral where they got the drop on George Chapman, the owner. They spent only a few moments selecting horses and saddled their mounts. Cleveland chose an unbroken mount, which threw him just outside the corral, so he swung aboard behind another man and the party fled north toward the Piños Altos Mountains, their final destination being Mexico.

One of the local citizens, John C. Jackson, realized what was happening and followed the fleeing men from a safe distance while a posse was being formed, which included Joseph N. Lafferr, Frank Andrews, Thomas E. Park and Dan Coomer. The advance posse joined Jackson and a running gunfight continued for 5 miles. Meanwhile Deputy Tom Hall organized a larger posse including Deputy U.S. Marshal Louis C. Kennon, Deputy Sheriff F. C. Cantley, and quite a number of citizens. When the reinforcements caught up with the forward posse, the fugitives saw that they were in trouble and their horses were tiring. When a shot killed Chavez, the rest of the gang dismounted and took refuge in a brushy canyon, and the battle continued for over an hour as each side fired every time a target presented itself. Cleveland was killed in the shooting and Lee was seriously, but not fatally, wounded. Taggart called out that he was ready to surrender and was joined by Spencer as they stepped out with arms raised. Lee was incapable of coming out or fighting but he surrendered as well, and the posse had to carry him to a wagon that had been brought out from town.

There seemed to be no sign of Joy, but he was afoot, so the posse began scouring the hills and ravines to find him. Posse man Lafferr, the widowed father of six children, rode through the brush looking for some sign when Joy suddenly rose up from behind, not 10 feet away, and fired both barrels of his shotgun into the man's back. Lafferr fell to the ground and died within minutes. The rest of the posse took cover again, allowing Joy to escape through the heavy brush. After an extended period of silence, the posse recovered Lafferr's body and again looked for the fugitive. When there was no sign of him, they loaded the wagon with the bodies of Lafferr, Chavez, and Cleveland and of prisoners Lee, Taggart, and Spencer and started for town.

The posse had not gone far before they halted and held a people's court in the middle of the road. They were angry at the killing of Lafferr and were determined to exact justice on their live prisoners, but after some discussion it was decided that Spencer should be returned to his cell while Lee and Taggart would be hanged.

While the men looked for an appropriate tree, a U.S. marshal arrived and intervened, but the men suggested he continue on to Fort Bayard and ask for directions on what should be done with the prisoners, and he agreed. After the U.S. marshal left, Deputy Sheriff Cantley strongly hinted to the men that he could not allow them to continue so long as he was armed, so they promptly disarmed him and continued to search for a sturdy limb and finally found a large piñon tree suitable for the work.

They removed Spencer from the wagon and moved the bodies of Chavez, Cleveland, and Lafferr to one side, pulled the wagon underneath the limb, and had Taggart stand while they held up Lee. The men positioned nooses around the necks of the men and bound the prisoners' feet, their hands already being tied. Lee, at that moment knowing his end was near, confessed to the killing of Webster and cleared Taggart of the crime, but the posse was angry over the killing of Lafferr, a crime of which both men were innocent, and the posse men whipped up the horses. The team rushed forward, and the two men were left dangling. Taggart struggled for some time but finally strangled to death, while Lee died with hardly a quiver due in part to the great loss of blood he had already experienced.

After life was extinct, the bodies were cut down and loaded into the wagon with the other three bodies. Spencer was again put aboard, and the wagon was driven to town. When an inquest was held on the bodies of Cleveland, Lee, Taggart, and Chavez on March 14, the jury found "that the deceased came to their death by gun-shot wounds and other injuries inflicted by the sheriff's posse while in pursuit and endeavoring to recapture the prisoners after having broken jail by over-powering the guards and attempting to make their escape and committed 7 miles north of Silver City, Grant County, New Mexico on the 11th day of March 1884."

Following his narrow escape from the posse after murdering Lafferr, Joy went to the house of E. Smith at the mouth of Bear Canyon. At the point of his shotgun, he demanded food, which was supplied. He then discussed the end of his fellow robbers with Sam Houston and declared he would never be hanged. He next went down Bear Creek and stole some blankets and other supplies from Pete Jensen's cabin. Joy seemed on good terms with Houston, so lawmen asked him to negotiate a surrender. The proposal was presented to Joy who agreed to appear on Thursday to be arrested, but Joy did not show. Instead the fugitive went to the home of Allen Fraze and begged for food, was supplied, and then headed for the bottomland near the cabin of Rackety Smith.

He was seen by a man named McGuire who, with Smith and Sterling Ashby, formed a posse of three and went after Joy. They suddenly came upon him but claimed they were following the fresh tracks of a deer as a ploy to get out of range of his shotgun. When they were at a safe distance, they ordered his surrender. Joy had already become suspicious, so when the demand came, he turned to run. Smith fired one round from his rifle but missed. The next shot, however, hit Joy's left leg and shattered both bones below the knee. Joy collapsed and called out that he surrendered.

The three men captured Joy, bound his wound the best they could, and took him to Silver City, arriving at 1:30 A.M. Saturday. The delay in getting their prisoner to the city allowed the wound to fester and later that day Joy's leg was amputated below the knee. When this did not resolve the medical problem, soon afterwards he had to undergo another amputation as the stump was taken above the knee. Since quite a number of men claimed a portion of the rewards that had been offered, Whitehill, who had spent a substantial amount of his personal funds in the pursuit and lost his job as sheriff, was forced to file a suit. The court resolved the dispute and awarded amounts to eight men: Whitehill got $1,333; Perry, Best, and Simpson got $444 each; Park, Andrews, Jackson, and Coomer each got $500.

In July Joy was indicted by the Grant County grand jury, but there was little chance for a fair trial there, so a change of venue was granted to Kingston, in the newly formed Sierra County. Trial was held at the fall term of the court with his aged father and sisters in attendance each day. The defendant had just lost his brother in a terrible mining accident. All this seemed to weigh heavily on the jurors so, on November 20, 1884, they returned a verdict of guilty of second-degree murder in the killing of engineer Webster, and Joy was sentenced to life imprisonment. He was delivered to the territorial penitentiary on January 7, 1885. On April 6, 1889, Governor E. G. Ross commuted his life sentence to twenty years, and then a six-year campaign began in earnest to get him a pardon. On March 4, 1896, the commissioners recommended that Joy receive his pardon, and twelve days later it was granted by Governor W. T. Thornton. Joy, after his release, moved to Arizona where he was suspected of running a still, but was never charged with that offense. He died quietly of natural causes in 1928 at the age of fifty-nine.

CHAPTER SIX

"GOULD'S MONEY" AND THE CORNETT-WHITLEY GANG

It was 1849 when the cholera epidemic swept through St. Louis. The city had just secured a charter for a railroad "from St. Louis to the western boundary of Missouri and thence to the Pacific Ocean." However, it was all but abandoned in the face of the deadly disease. Then fire broke out on a steamboat and soon spread to twenty-two other boats docked at the wharfs of the city's business district. Before the conflagration could be stopped, it spread and burned down most of the business district, and it appeared that the city was doomed to financial ruin. But there was unbridled optimism in the West at that time, so the city was able to recover within a year.

With prosperity the Pacific Railroad experienced a rebirth. Much of central Missouri was then uncharted land, so the civil engineers surveyed five alternate routes for the railroad and submitted them for consideration. The U.S. Congress, which wanted a railroad to the Pacific but was unwilling to support its construction, forced the builders to rely upon state aid, so building did not commence until July 4, 1851. Land was purchased and the bed graded, but progress was slow since the route that had been selected required the excavation of two tunnels.

The first division of what would become the Missouri Pacific Railway Company, a mere 38 miles to Franklin, was completed in July

1853. Two years later it had only reached Jefferson City, and in 1858 the tracks had only been extended to Tipton. Isolated railroads were being built in many other parts of the South during the pre–Civil War period, but most of the building stopped when the South seceded from the Union.

After the hostilities ended, building began again, slowly at first, but 1873 saw some major changes and a new interest in extending and connecting the tracks of many small railroads. In that year New Yorker Jay Gould acquired a substantial interest in the Union Pacific Railroad and then purchased a controlling interest in the Kansas Pacific, Denver Pacific, and Central Pacific companies. He soon acquired the controlling interest in the Missouri Pacific, the major competition for his Union Pacific Railroad, and assembled the "southwestern system" of rail lines. He continued to buy other railroad companies and added their trackage and rolling stock to his system, and by the early 1880s had extended his influence to Texas's railway companies. Gould, possibly more than other railroad millionaires, was hated by the common man. When desperate men targeted his trains for robbery or wreck, those responsible were more likely to be celebrated than incarcerated.

In February 1887 Brackett "Brack" Cornett and Bill Whitley proposed that they gather a group of good men and go to Flatonia to rob the Sunset train. On May 10 the party, which assembled at the graveyard outside Flatonia, consisted of Cornett, Whitley, John Barbour, Charley Ross, Ike Cloud, Edward Reeves, and Jim "Bud" Powell.

A fire was to be built along the tracks to signal the boys onboard that all was in readiness and mark the spot for them to stop the train— the place where the rest of the gang and the horses waited. Cornett, Whitley, and Reeves walked from the fire back to the station and were ready to board the train at Flatonia. It was their job to climb over the tender and capture the engine. However, a freight train was traveling just ahead of the passenger train, and Cornett was afraid that those on the freight train might see, by their bonfire signal, that a robbery was about to occur and would telegraph the alarm back to Flatonia from the next station. A posse could then have been mobilized before the robbers had

Brackett "Brack" Cornett
WESTERN HISTORY COLLECTIONS, UNIVERSITY OF OKLAHOMA LIBRARIES

a chance to complete their work and escape, so the passenger train was allowed to pass on to its destination unmolested. The three men at the station walked back to the fire and the gang rode off empty-handed.

Cornett and Whitley were determined to rob a train, so they turned their attention to McNeill Junction, about 12 miles north of Austin. They began to gather near McNeill on May 15 and watched to see what time the train passed. There were nearly a dozen men in the party when they arrived at the station on May 18, 1887, and overpowered the agent and passenger Riggles, who was the only man waiting to board at that station. Cornett broke the telegraph instrument and robbed Riggles while they awaited the arrival of the Missouri Pacific train. When the train stopped to let off passengers, Barbour with a Winchester rifle and Cornett with six-guns, covered the engineer and fireman while Powell went further down and covered the passenger cars with his rifle. Ross then threw ties onto the tracks in front of the engine and broke open the door to the express car. Some of the robbers fired their guns into the ceiling of the passenger cars to prevent the passengers from interfering and, though they did not intend to hurt anyone, traveling salesman Harry Landa received a wound in his arm.

The robbers were not interested in going through the passengers, so as soon as the door to the express car was forced open, Cornett, Whitley, and Reeves entered, and the two messengers surrendered without resistance. The robbers demanded the money from the safe. When messenger A. J. Northacker handed over one small package of currency, Cornett clubbed him with his pistol barrel and threatened to kill him, but he was convinced by Whitley not to shoot the messenger. The safe was cleaned out, the take being about $4,000. Then mail clerk Robert Spaulding told the robbers that there was no registered mail aboard as it had been sent on the daytime run. Cornett replied that it was all right as they were not after "Uncle Sam's money. We only want Gould's money."

The robbers removed the obstruction from the tracks and bid the trainmen a "pleasant good night" before they rode off into the darkness. After riding one-half mile, they built a fire and divided the money so quickly that it was not equally divided among the men, and they separated into smaller parties with Barbour and Whitley going together, Ross and Cloud in another party, and Cornett, Powell, and Reeves in the third party.

On June 1 the men gathered and again began to plan the robbery of a train at Flatonia, which was located halfway between Houston and San Antonio in Fayette County. There were again seven men interested, including Cornett, Whitley, Barbour, Ross, Powell, Reeves, and Will Jacobs, replacing Ike Cloud. They started for Flatonia, but Jacobs weakened and withdrew, leaving six men to do the work. The robbers separated some distance from the station after agreeing to meet at the graveyard a mile from town on Wednesday night, June 16, 1887. They planned to assault the train on Thursday, but Cornett and Barbour failed to board the train as scheduled, so the date for the robbery was moved ahead.

On Friday, June 18, as the eastbound train pulled out of Flatonia, two men armed with six-shooters and disguised with false beards swung aboard the "blind baggage" of the express car just behind the tender. They climbed over and got the drop on engineer B. A. Pickens and his fireman and then ordered the engineer to continue until they told him to stop. When the train reached a bonfire near a bridge ahead, the robbers ordered Pickens to stop. The engineer later said he could see four men, all disguised with beards and masks, in the firelight from the bonfire, but later it was suggested that as many as a dozen men might have been involved, including William Humphreys and Tom Jones, whose alias was Montgomery. The gang first broke into the express car and mail car, taking everything of value, and again Cornett found a reason to pistol whip the messenger. While the men were preoccupied with the safes, messengers, and mail clerk, the engineer slipped away and passed the word to the passengers to hide their valuables. Cornett, Whitley, and Powell next went through the cars, stripping all the passengers of their valuables and clubbing any who hesitated, though many had hidden the bulk of their possessions. All the while Cornett, who seemed to be in charge, sucked on a candy stick.

At one point Barbour called out, "We have been here long enough. Come on, Dick," a prearranged alias intended to later confuse lawmen.

In the South those in charge of any operation were commonly referred to as the "Captain," so the newspapers labeled Cornett "Captain Dick," and one newspaper went so far as suggesting he be called "Captain Dick with the candy stick." The gang took their plunder, mounted their horses, and rode off into the night. At daybreak they were more than 20 miles from Flatonia, so they stopped and counted their take, which totaled $7,009.50 and lots of jewelry. All was divided as equally as possible, and the gang separated into smaller parties and rode off in different directions.

It was not long before Cornett and Whitley began planning the robbery of a bank. They looked into the banks at Fredericksburg and Cuero, but in both cases they thought there were rangers in town and backed out. About three weeks later, probably feeling the pressure from state officials and the public to identify and capture them, they decided to permanently divide into three pairs of robbers and divide the state as well, with Cornett and Milt Day (who replaced Ross) working the southern part, Barbour and Whitley covering north Texas, and Reeves and Powell leaving the state on an extended spree. The latter pair had some difficulty in Arkansas and were arrested but not identified, so when they were released they started for Texas.

Reeves's niece mentioned that her "Uncle Ed" was coming for a visit, so Sheriff Boyd of Johnson County was notified and laid a trap to capture Reeves. He left a deputy on watch with specific instructions to take no action when Reeves arrived, but to notify him so that he could muster a posse to make the arrest. The deputy, possibly seeing the large reward before him, decided to make the arrest himself. Reeves got out of the house and, though he had received a bullet wound in his leg, managed to get away and hide in a cornfield. The sheriff arrived later that day and took the trail of the fugitive, following it to a stand of timber at sunset where he and Reeves exchanged shots. In the morning the trail was followed again, and Reeves was found lying in a creek bed, weakened from the loss of blood from the leg wound and a fresh wound where a bullet grazed a deep furrow in his forehead. He was arrested and taken to San Antonio. Cornett and Whitley twice planned to rescue Reeves, but both times fate intervened and Reeves was tried and convicted. Powell, hearing of Reeves's situation, fled into the Arizona Territory and was not heard of in Texas for several years.

Cornett and Milt Day enlisted Henry John Kelly and Jim Herin to flesh out their new gang and rode toward Harris County where they planned to rob the Houston & Texas Central train at Gum Island. Along the way they stole fresh horses as they were needed, and word reached Sheriff Ellis that four heavily armed horse thieves were active on the border of his county. He formed a posse and came upon the robbers' camp near Houston, where they shot it out with Kelly, Day, and Herin, but the three men escaped. Cornett had gone into Houston to buy ammunition, and when he was returning to camp, he encountered a deputy sheriff and the farmer who owned the horse on which he was mounted. Before the farmer could alert the deputy, Cornett spurred his horse to a gallop and escaped under a hail of bullets. Day and Kelly returned to their homes in Gonzales County, where they were arrested and taken back to Harris County, and confessed to the Gum Island Plan. However, they could be tried only for horse theft and were convicted and sentenced to serve terms at the Huntsville prison with Day getting seventeen and Kelly seven years.

Cornett returned to Karnes County where he was joined by Herin and recruited John Ensall for their gang. They decided it was time for a bold engagement, so they started for the Great Northern train station a few miles from Austin, where they planned to rob both the northbound and southbound trains. They camped near the town of Manchaca, and Ensall went after supplies. Ex-Ranger Jim Martin, who had been notified to watch for the gang members, arrested Ensall and formed a posse to go after Cornett and Herin. There was an exchange of shots, but the two fugitives escaped, leaving behind three pistols, $140, and the hands of cards they were playing when the posse arrived. Cornett believed they had been betrayed by Ensall and, not knowing what he might have told the authorities, the two fugitives fled into Mexico where they remained until it seemed safe to return. In December Ensall managed to escape with another desperate character named Joe Penton, while his partners were south of the border, and he was not seen again.

Cornett and Herin finally returned to U.S. soil and on the evening of February 12, 1888, Cornett went to the Frio County home of Alf Allee, a man who had previously been a supporter of Cornett. The following day Allee notified the authorities to come to his house and collect the body of Cornett and explained, "Cornett came to my house one night, got supper and went away; then he came back the next morning [February 12th] and was standing by a fire in the yard warming himself. I leveled my pistol and called on Cornett to surrender. The outlaw replied, 'Not by a d__ sight,' and got off two shots, but I was too quick."

There were three bullet holes in Cornett's body, two in the breast and one in the forehead, all entering from the front, a fourth shot reportedly had gone wild, and there were powder burns on the face of the deceased, which showed the two men were very close to one another when the shoot-out occurred. Allee showed his hat where a bullet from Cornett was supposed to have made a hole, but he claimed that there was no one present to confirm his story except a young Mexican boy. His version of the affray held up under scrutiny and rewards were paid by Wells, Fargo & Company, the Southern Pacific and Missouri Pacific Railroads, the Pacific Express Company, and the state of Texas. The postal service refused to pay its reward as it was for arrest and conviction and not "dead or alive." Soon after Cornett was killed, Will Jacobs surrendered, but he was not tried for his part in the Flatonia train robbery.

While Cornett and his gang were busy in the south, Whitley and Barbour moved into the north part of Texas. Their first crime was the murder of Deputy Sheriff W. J. Stanley in Williamson County on August 6, 1887. Stanley had been persistent in his pursuit of the robbers, and after they had disposed of him, the two men escaped into the Indian Territory where they recruited two desperadoes. The gang of four, which now included Kep Queen and E. C. Foster, whose alias was Stephens, robbed the Cisco Bank in Eastland County and divided $10,000 in currency.

On Christmas morning they tried to rob the southbound Missouri, Kansas, and Texas train at Atoka in the Choctaw Nations and managed to drive the messenger from the express car, but there was nothing of value inside and the robbers left empty-handed. On June 15, 1888, the boys robbed the southbound "Katy" at the Verdigris Bridge in the Creek Nation but only got $8 and some cheap jewelry. On July 2 the Fredericksburg bank was robbed of $300 by two masked men, probably Whitley and Barbour.

Soon afterwards lawmen learned of the hiding place of Whitley and Barbour in the Indian Territories, but when the posse arrived they found the men had vacated their camp hours earlier. The two fugitives next tried to hide in Lampasas County but Sheriff Reynolds was alerted to their presence in his jurisdiction and organized a posse. They engaged the two fugitives in a running fight for several weeks. Whitley wanted to make a stand, but Barbour refused, so they parted company. Barbour fled east and was driven by a posse into the Louisiana swamps, while Whitley went southwest to territory more familiar to him.

Will and Eli Harrell had been jailed in Karnes County on February 17, 1888, for harboring the wanted men, but Will was released on bond. Soon there came news of an attempt to rob the Sunset train at Harwood in Gonzales County, which was 75 miles east of San Antonio and only 15 miles from Flatonia, but this had been a trap and the express and mail cars were filled with armed men.

When the train pulled out of Harwood at dusk on September 22, 1888, two masked men climbed over the tender and captured engineer Dan Toomey and his fireman. After traveling a short distance, they stopped the train and had the fireman uncouple the back of the train. The trainmen, however, had not been informed of the plan, and the fireman cleverly separated the train between the combined baggage and mail and the express cars. As a result, the train proceeded forward with only the postal car, and most of the lawmen were left with the back of the train. When they stopped the train, the two men in the engine were joined by Sam Neff and probably the two Harrell brothers. They saw that the express car had been detached, so they went back to the mail car with engineer Toomey as a shield. They forced him through the door where Deputy U.S. Marshal Duval "Bud" West fired his shotgun at the dark figure in the doorway, tearing away the engineer's cheek. The robbers next pushed the fireman through the door, but the next shotgun blast missed its target. The robbers then departed in haste, empty-handed.

When the Harwood trap failed, another plan for the capture of Whitley was devised. Whitley was to be lured to the home of Will Harrell on the edge of Floresville, a little town south of San Antonio on the San Antonio & Aransas Pass Railway. U.S. Marshal Rankin took three trusted deputies to the house, and they took up their hiding places to wait, Rankin in the back room and the others outside. At a late hour Harrell and Whitley arrived, and Harrell lighted the lamp, a signal to the lawmen, while Whitley took a seat at the table and laid his Winchester rifle across his knees. Marshal Rankin suddenly appeared in the door with his scattergun leveled at Whitley and ordered him to surrender, but Whitley tried to raise his rifle and Rankin fired both barrels. This was the signal for his deputies to rush in, but when they arrived they found Whitley riddled with twenty buckshot pellets and already dead. Whitley's remains were taken to San Antonio, identified, and turned over to his wife, who took the body back to Lampasas County for burial. Cornett and Whitley had met a violent end, but what happened to the rest of the gang?

Tom Jones was arrested in September 1887, pled guilty to the Flatonia train robbery, and was sentenced to serve five years in prison.

Barbour, Queen, and Foster were found in the Cherokee Nation on November 16, 1888. Queen was killed resisting arrest. Foster, alias Stephens, and Barbour escaped, but Foster was captured a year later and extradited to Texas, tried for the Cisco bank robbery, and sentenced to serve ten years in prison at Huntsville. Within a few weeks after Foster's capture, Barbour was cornered and shot to death when he resisted arrest.

Ed Reeves, though he had provided a detailed confession and cooperated with the authorities, was tried in February 1889, convicted, and given a life sentence to be served at Detroit's House of Corrections.

Sam Neff, the only man arrested for the Harwood train robbery, was never tried for that offense or for the put-up charge of stealing a horse from Eli Harrell, and he was set free.

Eli Harrell disappeared soon after the death of Whitley, and it was rumored that he had been murdered by members of the gang for his part in betraying Whitley. There was never any proof of foul play but he was never heard from again. His brother, Will, was sent to a federal prison where he reportedly died in 1892.

James Powell avoided arrest for several years by fleeing to Arizona, and then to Montana, but he was finally tracked down and returned to Texas in 1892. In late February 1893 Powell pled guilty to mail robbery in the Texas circuit court and was sentenced to a term in a federal prison.

George Brown, John Cresswell, and Alexander Lewis were tried for various crimes and acquitted.

Ike Cloud and Charley Ross, early members of the Cornett-Whitley Gang, disappeared from the records of Texas justice and, living under aliases, were never heard of again. William Humphreys was in jail on the last day of January 1888 and then is suddenly absent from the records of Texas criminal law and the newspapers. Ensall and Herin were believed to be in hiding in the Texas backcountry, but without leadership they were considered harmless so little effort was expended to bring them to justice. They were never arrested for crimes committed by the gang.

Joe Bennett and Newton Butler, supporters of the Cornett-Whitley Gang with the latter being the man who supplied them with false beards, were never arrested.

Alfred Allee and John Rankin, the two men responsible for the final chapter in the lives of the gang leaders, lived for another decade before Allee was killed in August 1896 and Rankin was shot to death in November 1897.

CHAPTER SEVEN

CANYON OF THE DEVIL

The Atlantic & Pacific Railroad Company was chartered by an act of Congress in 1866 to build a railroad from Springfield, Missouri, through Indian Territory, finally ending in San Francisco. The track laying was planned to follow the thirty-fifth parallel along the route surveyed by the Army in 1853. A large number of investors were led by John C. Fremont, and their first acquisition was the bankrupt South West Branch of the Pacific Railroad, which had laid its tracks to Rolla by 1860. The railroad was built from Rolla westward through the northern part of New Mexico and into northern Arizona Territory. When the tracks reached the Canyon of the Devil, known by its Spanish name Canyon Diablo, the building continued to the west but trains stopped rolling beyond the canyon until a bridge could be constructed across the 225-foot-deep gorge.

In early 1881 the undertaking to build a steel bridge was so immense that a town was laid out on the east rim and named for the canyon. The heavy stone abutments were constructed in mid-1881 but it was not until July 1, 1882, that the last piece of iron was installed. When the 580-foot-long trestle was completed, much of the town was disassembled and moved to the next end-of-track, more than 100 miles west,

414 Larimer Street, Denver, Colo.

Train crossing the Canyon Diablo
DENVER PUBLIC LIBRARY, WESTERN HISTORY COLLECTION, Z-3428

while the remainder was left to deteriorate. All through the western portion of northern Arizona, ties and rails had been moved into place so that westward construction could continue at a rapid pace. By 1889 there was nothing left of the town of Canyon Diablo except the station and trading post, a warehouse, and loading pens. It had been one of the roughest towns in Arizona during its heyday but had died a quiet death as soon as the first train rolled across the canyon westward.

Northern Arizona Territory, where Canyon Diablo was located, was cattle country, and one of the largest ranches in the region was owned by the Aztec Land and Cattle Company, known as the Hashknife outfit. During the last months of 1888, the weather grew very cold, and the work was all but finished for the year. The cowboys who stayed on through the winter tried whatever diversions they could invent to pass the long hours while waiting the arrival of spring. One evening in late February, two of the men stepped onto the porch to watch the sun set and, being bored, Daniel M. Harvick said to John H. "J. J." Smith, "Smitty, let's go and rob a train or open a real estate office. Anything decent and honest. I'm tired of working day and night through the spring, and summer and fall, stealing cattle for someone else and then waiting all winter for the chance to do it all over again."

Train robbery almost seemed a profession in those days because so many infamous men had taken an interest in the work, and a few, it was believed, had gotten rich at it. Smith looked at his partner for a moment and then agreed to go along.

While they were discussing their plans, two other cowboys joined them on the porch. After hearing their ideas for excitement, John "Long John" Halford and William D. Stiren, often misspelled Starin or Sterin, dealt themselves in. Within a few minutes all four men had perfected their initial plan to rob the Atlantic & Pacific express at Canyon Diablo Station. They spent a week leaving the ranch one at a time, to divert later suspicion, and rendezvoused in the Shovelin Hills where they discussed in detail the role each man would play in the robbery. They broke camp on March 19, 1889, and rode to a point 2 miles above the station and waited there for the sun to set. Once it was sufficiently dark to hide their movements, they moved to within 200 yards of the station, tied their horses to trees there, and hunkered down to wait for the train. The eastbound No. 2 whistled as it reached the bridge just before 11:00 P.M., crossed, and then stopped at the station to fill its wood box.

As soon as the train came to a halt, the fireman stepped down on the south side and began checking the undercarriage of the engine. The robbers, with handkerchiefs over their faces and hats pulled down, had split into pairs with Harvick and Stiren on the south, so they stepped up

William O. "Buckey" O'Neill and his posse
SHARLOT HALL MUSEUM, PRESCOTT, ARIZONA

to the fireman and took him hostage. On the north side Smith and Halford were busy getting the drop on engineer Charles Woods and bringing him around the train to the south side. Smith stuck the muzzle of his six-shooter into Woods's stomach and ordered him to go to the express car and demand entrance. The engineer complied, and after a moment's delay the door slid open. Agent E. G. Knickerbocker stared down at the four armed men as Smith ordered him to climb down and then warned him not to "try something."

The boys were taken aback when the agent said, in a disconcertingly friendly manner, "Why, hello boys" and climbed down without hesitation.

Smith told the others to shoot the agent if he had any trouble inside and then climbed aboard. He found the car empty of people, but saw there the two safes he expected to find. When Smith announced the coast was clear, Harvick pushed the agent back into the car where Smith ordered him to open the safes. Knickerbocker said, pointing to the larger through safe, "I can't open that safe. There's a time lock on it that's set for Santa Fe."

Smith accepted his explanation but demanded he open the local safe. While it was being opened, Harvick climbed into the car. The two men cleaned out all the valuables—including a large pile of currency, rolls of coins, and handfuls of jewelry—and put the plunder into sacks. They carried their treasure to their horses, pushing the engineer and fireman ahead, mounted, and told the hostages they could then return to the train.

The four men rode 5 miles before they stopped, built a fire in a cedar grove, and spread the loot on the ground. As they sorted through the jewelry, they tried to separate it into four piles of approximately equal value and also divided the currency and coin equally. To be certain that none could complain that he had a short share, Harvick was blindfolded and his hand was placed on a pile, and he would say whose it was, so that the assignment of each cache to each robber was done blindly. The men would later say that they had gotten only $7,000, but the reported loss by the express company was set at more than $40,000 with some estimates as high as $150,000. Each man buried a substantial portion of his share, particularly the identifiable jewelry items, and they agreed to come back together at a later time to collect it. They also buried their rifles and concealed their six-shooters in their waistbands to appear as unarmed travelers. Once the treasure was apportioned and buried, the men separated into parties of two to leave two separate trails and confuse any posses out looking for a party of four armed train robbers. They decided to meet at a predesignated place in Wyoming, and then Harvick and Stiren headed for the San Francisco Peaks and the Black Falls of the Little Colorado River while Halford and Smith turned their horses north and headed for the river above Canyon Diablo in Navajo country.

When Stiren and Harvick reached the Little Colorado River 40 miles away, they found it a muddy flood of swirling ice and debris, but they had no choice but to cross. They stripped and carefully rolled their clothes into a bundle inside their slickers to try to keep them dry for the other side. They spurred their horses into the freezing water and were carried down river by the current, but fought their way along until they finally made the other side. Although everything—men, horses and bundles—was under water several times, the clothes remained dry. Once on the opposite bank, they dressed, mounted, and rode on toward Lee's Ferry, the only safe place to cross the larger Colorado River. They stopped for a day to let their horses graze and rest and then rode to within a few miles of the ferry. For the first time since they had split the treasure, they felt safe enough to build a fire and cook a hot meal. After a good night's rest, they rode to the rim of the Grand Canyon above the ferry, waited until dark, muffled the horses' feet, led them onto the ferry, and crossed into Utah.

Smith and Halford had crossed the Little Colorado River at Wolf's Ferry, resupplied at the trading post, and also headed for Lee's Ferry. Because their route had been easier, they arrived at the ferry a day ahead of Harvick and Stiren and crossed into Utah.

Not far from the river was Wah Weep, located 5 miles from Cannonville, a settlement of polygamous Mormons in hiding from federal lawmen. Bigamy had been a federal offense since the U.S. Congress passed the Morrill Act in 1862, but that law, though upheld by the Supreme Court, had proven ineffective in stopping the Mormon practice of plural marriage. In 1882 Congress tried to correct the weakness in the Morrill Act by passing the Edmunds Act making "bigamous cohabitation" a misdemeanor that could result in a prison sentence and disenfranchisement. Smith and Halford found a log cabin at Wah Weep that looked promising and stopped to ask for food and lodging, and the old Mormon was more than accommodating. They believed they would be safe there as word of the robbery could not have gotten ahead of them, and their hosts were also fugitives from the law.

The following day Harvick and Stiren arrived at the same cabin, entirely by coincidence, and when the old Mormon took them to the stable, to their surprise, they found Smith's and Halford's horses. They cared for their animals and then went to the house, where they greeted their partners in crime as strangers. After dinner, beds were made on the cabin floor for Harvick and Halford while Smith and Stiren were put up in a granary attached to the stable. The next morning Harvick heard men talking outside the cabin and awoke Halford. Still not suspicious, they opened the door to find themselves covered with cocked rifles in the hands of four Mormons. Another party of Mormons milling around the granary called for the prisoners to be brought down. When all was ready, an elder of the church, who was also the justice of the peace, entered the granary to capture Smith and Stiren. When he tried to wake them, however, he found himself their prisoner. Smith soon traded their valuable hostage for Halford and Harvick and their horses and made their getaway.

It seemed impossible to the boys that anyone could be close on their trails, considering the course they took and the obstacles they had overcome, but while the Mormons were trying to capture the train robbers, a posse had arrived in Cannonville, its leader having been sent for. William Owen "Buckey" O'Neill, sheriff of Yavapai County, had earned his sobriquet bucking the tiger at the faro tables of Prescott, Arizona, the county seat. He had formed his posse of hand-picked men including A&P's special agent Carl Holton, Deputy James L. Black, and Special Deputy Ed St. Clair. They had quickly got on the track of one pair and, realizing by their direction where they were heading, they hurried on to Lee's Ferry and into Utah. As soon as O'Neill received word that the robbers had been captured, the posse mounted and rode south. When they arrived at Wah Weep, however, the robbers had fled, so they deputized several of the Mormons, and the party took the trail.

The fugitives traveled overnight and the next day killed a beef and made camp. The following day they started for the tanks near Lee's Ferry, all the time with O'Neill and his posse close behind. When the boys stopped for the night, the posse passed them by and set up an ambush.

When the boys came to the rim of a deep canyon on one side, they noticed men dodging among the pines and juniper trees on the other side, trying to get into position to capture them, so they were in effect surrounded and had ridden into a trap. The lawmen began calling for their surrender, O'Neill introducing himself to them, and several of the deputies began shooting with rifles. When Halford and Stiren saw the officers, Indian trailers, and deputized Mormons firing, they returned fire with their six-guns, but the posse was out of range for pistols. Smith and Harvick dismounted and led their horses as they searched for a place to go down the steep canyon sides but finally had to take refuge in the rocks. The exchange continued until Halford and Stiren, seeing further resistance futile, surrendered.

While the posse was busy capturing their partners, Smith and Harvick managed to climb down and escape on foot. The two fugitives continued toward the tanks near Lee's Ferry and walked all night and the next day, resting periodically by taking one-hour turns sleeping or watching. Since their boots were made for riding, walking began to hurt their feet. They would walk barefoot until the cold forced them to put the boots on again, By changing their footgear on and off, they managed to get to the tanks, which had been their original destination after leaving Wah Weep.

They were at the tanks only an hour when the posse arrived, so the two men laid down among the rocks to hide. They thought that if they could stay hidden and get up the canyon, dodging among the rocks and occasional brush, they might again escape, but when Smith made his first move, he was seen and had to surrender or be shot. As soon as Harvick saw Smith in custody, he ran for the canyon. He had it in mind to get across the river and head for Mexico, but he was weak from cold, hunger, and lack of sleep. Lawmen on fresh horses caught him easily on the level, open ground. As soon as the two prisoners and all the deputies were in camp, a beef was found and slaughtered, and a fire built to warm them and cook the food. The party then started back to the place where Halford and Stiren had been captured and were at that time being guarded by several deputized Mormons.

O'Neill decided that taking the men back to Prescott on horseback provided too great a chance for escape, so a wagon was brought up and the prisoners loaded aboard. They were taken to the Union Pacific station at Millford where they boarded a train for Salt Lake City. There the requisition papers were secured and the lawmen and their prisoners started for Denver where they would board the train for Arizona by way of New Mexico.

Once the four train robbers were in the Denver jail, the posse men and their thrilling chase were celebrated in Denver. The men imbibed to excess. When they boarded the train for Albuquerque, New Mexico, the next day, the prisoners were shackled at the ankles, but O'Neill removed the handcuffs so they could travel comfortably and assigned a deputy to guard them. It was Holton's turn on watch and, as soon as the deputy dozed, the men began to experiment with their chains. Smith found he could remove one ankle cuff by removing his boot, and he tucked the loose chain in his waistband. None of the others could remove their shackles, so they helped him get through a window and escape while the train was traveling at full speed.

When the escape was discovered, the train was stopped and backed to the point where it was thought Smith had jumped. The area was searched, but the escapee was not found. The other three men made it to the Prescott jail safely on April 15, 1889.

Smith hid out for two months while posses searched the area for him, first a posse led by Arizona deputies Holton and Black and then by New Mexico lawmen. When interest in him seemed to wane, he decided it was his chance to make it into Texas, but he made a mistake when he found a settler's horse staked out and stole it. A posse was soon on the trail of the horse thief, not yet knowing the desperate character they were after, and followed Smith into Texas where they overtook him. When Smith tried to outrun the posse, he was shot in the hip and captured. After he was in custody, he was identified as the train robber wanted in Arizona. On June 3, 1899, O'Neill received a telegram that Smith had been captured, so he hurried to Texas and brought him back to Prescott on June 8.

The prisoners were tried at the summer session of the court and convicted of robbing a train, which at the time was a capital offense in Arizona. However, probably at the urging of the railroad and express company, they were spared death sentences because the plunder had not yet been recovered and there was still hope that the men would turn it over. Halford, Harvick, and Stiren were sentenced to serve twenty-five years and Smith received thirty years at the Territorial Prison near Yuma. Harvick and Halford arrived at the infamous prison on July 22, 1889, and were registered as Nos. 590 and 592 respectively; Stiren arrived on July 28 and registered as prisoner No. 594. July was the hottest month of the year, when temperatures in that region could reach 120 degrees, but Smith did not suffer those temperatures that year as his arrival was delayed until November 24 when he was registered as prisoner No. 621.

On August 13, 1893, Governor Louis C. Hughes pardoned Smith, the man with the longest sentence, after he'd served only four years. When he failed to lead detectives to the buried treasure, Harvick was pardoned by Governor Benjamin Joseph Franklin on December 25, 1896, after serving seven years, but again the train robber steered clear of the treasure cache. Stiren and Halford were pardoned on November 1, 1897, after serving eight years, but they did not go for the treasure either. Smith and Harvick were watched until 1904 when the express company finally gave up hope of ever recovering the buried treasure.

Upon his release John Halford moved to El Paso, Texas, but he was terribly ill from the plague contracted during his final days in prison and died soon after gaining his freedom.

William Stiren joined the army's expedition to Cuba under an alias and was killed in the charge on San Juan Hill in 1898. William "Buckey" O'Neill was killed in that same battle. O'Neill's remains were finally brought back to America and buried at Arlington Cemetery on May 1, 1899.

John "J. J." Smith was living in Pennsylvania after his pardon, destitute and working at odd jobs when he could find one. One day he announced that he was heading west on a business venture and, when he returned several months later, drove a herd of 300 head of cattle to the new ranch he had just purchased. He prospered as a rancher and lived out the rest of his life in comfort.

Daniel Harvick, the other surviving train robber, was in Arizona when Smith went west and about the same time also seemed to come into some money. He claimed to have done some ranching, prospecting, and a variety of other jobs to explain his financial situation. He too lived out the remainder of his life in comfort.

CHAPTER EIGHT

ROSCOE'S SWITCH

David Boone was born in Iowa on November 3, 1871, but his family of three brothers and one sister moved to Hill City, South Dakota, when he was quite young. Boone was a restless, adventurous youth and tired of his quiet home life, so he left home and headed south. He was not wanted for any crime but he adopted the alias William Thompson, and because of his youthful appearance, the sobriquet "Kid" was soon added by the cowboys with whom he worked. Thereafter he always went by his alias, and it would take clever detective work to uncover his true identity.

In 1888 Thompson met the Fox brothers near Prescott, Arizona, and the three men engaged in rustling in the Salt River Valley. When one of the Fox brothers was shot dead by the constable, the two remaining gang members fled into New Mexico where they recruited Dave Taylor as their new partner in a bank robbery. However, Thompson soon tired of his relationship with Fox and took on as his new sidekick John Long, with whom he returned to Arizona where they engaged in horse stealing. Both men were captured, tried, convicted, and sentenced to serve three-year terms in the infamous Territorial Prison near Yuma.

They arrived on November 2, 1889, and were released on March 20, 1892, having served only twenty-nine months. Thompson decided he needed to leave Arizona, where he was too well known, so he drifted into California. He met Alvarado "Alva" Johnson in October 1892 and took a job on his ranch working as a teamster and cowboy.

Alvarado Johnson was born in Gentry County, Missouri, in 1858. He moved to California in 1873 and settled with his parents, brothers, John and Cornelius, and sister, Olive, in Big Tujunga Canyon located in the San Gabriel Mountains east of the San Fernando Valley. In 1881 he started his own ranch in the canyon where he raised cattle and poultry and had done so well that he also opened a feed store in Los Angeles. In 1893 Johnson was thirty-five years old, married with two young children and two teenaged stepdaughters. Johnson had a good reputation in the canyon but was involved in water rights litigation with older brother John, and he felt he had a score to settle with the railroad because of its practice of setting excessive shipping fees that cut deeply into the profits of ranchers and farmers. He had on his ranch an old man named George Smith who did menial tasks about the house in return for room and board.

Thompson had not been turned from his lawless ways by his experiences in prison, so soon after his arrival at the Johnson ranch, he began figuring and interested Johnson in his plans.

On December 23, 1893, Southern Pacific's northbound train No. 20 arrived at Burbank's train station before 10:30 P.M. A constable saw four men dressed as tramps climb aboard the "blind baggage" of the express car just behind the tender and ordered them off. One tramp, Thompson in disguise, took off at a run with the constable in pursuit, but when the tramp disappeared into the darkness, the constable gave up the search. The three tramps who had not fled climbed aboard again while Thompson circled around and boarded the train from the opposite side, and the train left the station on schedule.

When the train reached Roscoe Switch, 4 miles north of Burbank, Thompson, with a bandana pulled up over his face, climbed over the tender and, with a six-shooter in each hand, got the drop on engineer William "Rocky Bill" Stewart and his fireman. He shouted, "Stop this

William "Billy" Milton Breakenridge, sheriff
WESTERN HISTORY COLLECTIONS, UNIVERSITY OF OKLAHOMA LIBRARIES

train," and fired his pistols to emphasize his resolve just as the engineer set the brakes, but the train suddenly swerved onto a blind siding as the switch had been thrown by Thompson's accomplice.

When the train was brought safely to a halt on the siding, the engineer saw a bright bonfire ahead and a second masked man, Johnson carrying a Winchester rifle, stepping out of the darkness.

Thompson ordered the engineer to get down, and just then the three stowaway tramps took off running and disappeared into the brush under a hail of bullets. A constable and brakemen, upon hearing the shots, walked forward to investigate, and the constable announced, "What is the meaning of this? I am an officer."

Thompson replied, "Get back there. . . . Get back now, will you." He then fired a warning shot as the two inquisitive men retreated.

The two robbers used Stewart and the fireman as a shield and herded them to the express car door. They made no demand for the door to be opened but instead placed a small can of black powder against the door and had the engineer light the short fuse. When it exploded, it blew a large hole in the door and knocked messenger Fred Potts senseless. By the time Potts recovered and realized the situation, the two robbers and the trainmen were already in the car. Thompson ordered the messenger to open the safe, which he did, and when the young bandit saw the contents, he said sarcastically, "She's as full as a daisy, ain't she?"

Potts handed over $150 from the safe, all it contained, and Thompson then asked for the through safe. When told by Potts that his car did not have one, Johnson tried to scare the messenger by mentioning an incident where a messenger was killed trying to protect the treasure in his care. However, Potts replied that it happened in the East, "where they carry lots of treasure. We don't have it on the coast."

The two robbers accepted Potts's explanation and herded the three trainmen out of the express car and toward the engine. Thompson then ordered Stewart to pull the engine forward through the barricade until it ran off the end of track. Roscoe Station was a small depot with pens for loading cattle on a blind siding 100 yards to the south. The siding had a barricade of railroad ties at the end and just beyond that was a ditch 6 feet deep. Stewart asked that they reconsider and offered to go with them and wait until they left, and they agreed to his proposal. They took Stewart some distance from the engine and then, to prevent him from seeing their horses, ordered him to stop and wait for a signal. Then they walked off into the darkness. In a few minutes there was a single shot, and the engineer returned to his train. He backed the train onto the main line, threw the switch, and went into San Fernando, where he reported the robbery.

Southern Pacific's detective Will Smith assembled a posse but had trouble finding horses for all his men, so their start for the scene was delayed until 4:00 A.M. The posse found the trail of the fleeing bandits heading northeast, and from all the circumstances Smith was certain the robbers were "green hands." He believed they had gone out from Los Angeles, probably had returned there, and had disappeared among the town's questionable characters, so the lawmen concentrated their investigation on watching anyone suspicious.

Wells, Fargo & Company had a standard reward of $300 for each robber, and the Southern Pacific Railroad offered a reward of $1,000 for information leading to the arrest of the robbers. The description sent out read, "One man about 5 feet 9 inches in height, weight about 175 pounds, wore dark colored cape over coat, white hat and light moustache. The other about the same height, weight about 160 pounds."

The search continued from the scene of the robbery, and detective Smith asked San Bernardino County Undersheriff John C. King to bring his bloodhounds to the scene and try to pick up the scent. King took his two dogs to the scene by special train and arrived on Sunday at 4:00 A.M., but it had rained heavily overnight so the dogs could not find a scent to follow and they returned home. After following up every clue, there was nothing to do but wait for some break in the case.

While the take had been small, the robbery and escape seemed a perfect success, so Thompson and Johnson decided to try again, hoping for a bigger haul. On February 15, 1894, train No. 20 left the Burbank depot with Engineer David W. Thomas at the throttle and Arthur Masters working as his fireman, but fireman Ben LaGrange was also in the cab, catching a ride home to San Fernando. Two tramps, nineteen-year-old Harry Daly and James R. Pacey, were stowed away on the engine pilot, the "cowcatcher" device on the front of the engine. Uncharacteristically, two fully loaded fruit cars had been coupled behind the tender and in front of the express car. As the train neared Roscoe Station, Thomas saw two men seated on the platform of the small station stand up as the train approached. One ignited a ball of rags soaked in some flammable fluid and threw it onto the tracks as a signal to stop, and both men yelled out, "Stop her! Stop her!" The two men then fired at the engine, one with a Winchester rifle and the other with two six-shooters.

Thomas warned the firemen to crouch low and hide from the gunfire and tried to accelerate to escape the danger, increasing his speed on the upgrade from 18 miles per hour. In the excitement Thomas did not notice that the switch had been thrown, but suddenly the train swerved onto the blind siding, which threw fireman Masters down into the opening between the tender beam and the firebox. Masters caught himself before he fell through and under the train's wheels. The brakes were set almost immediately, but it was too late to stop the speeding train before it reached the barricade of railroad ties. The engine went through the ties and into the ditch and dug into the earth nose down, as if trying to burrow its way underground. The tender crashed into the engine but remained upright. The two fruit cars, filled to capacity with oranges, crushed forward and then overturned. Masters's legs were still dangling between the engine and tender where they were crushed and pinned.

Thomas and LaGrange scrambled off the train as soon as it stopped and hid from the robbers, Thomas behind a large cactus from where he watched as the armed men rushed the engine. Masters was screaming for help, so LaGrange hurried to him and was about to begin cutting away the tender beam when he was taken hostage.

Pacey, one of the tramps riding on the cowcatcher, had been thrown clear and knocked unconscious. The cowcatcher had been folded under the engine by the force of the crash and the engine plowed a furrow 5 feet deep in the hard soil. The second tramp, Daly, was pinned onto the cowcatcher when it crashed through the barricade and was crushed to death beneath the locomotive.

LaGrange, at gunpoint, was marched to the express car where the robbers, without any demand or warning, put dynamite against the door and had LaGrange light the fuse. The bomb blew apart the doorplate, bottom rail, two door stiles and the fan wing on one door and shattered nine windows in the bulkhead inside the door; the door itself was still intact. Thompson, with two six-guns, and Johnson, with his Winchester rifle, fired several shots through the blast hole into the car while instructing the messenger, "Open quick or we'll blow you to hell!"

When messenger Harry Edgar opened the door, the robbers pushed LaGrange ahead as they entered. While Thompson went through the registered packages, Johnson periodically fired a shot down the side of the train to keep the passengers from interfering. Thompson found only $100 in U.S. currency, $1,200 in newly minted Mexican silver coins, and several other sacks of coins and asked, "Is this all you've got?"

When told it was all they had aboard, he ordered Edgar and LaGrange to carry the seven sacks of plunder weighing seventy-five pounds. There was a buckboard 200 yards from the tracks, but they'd gone only 100 yards, Thompson ordered the trainmen to put down the sacks and remain there, to keep them from getting a good look at the team and wagon. LaGrange then told Thompson that the fireman was trapped in the cab and Thompson said, "Damn the luck. If I'd known this would happen I wouldn't have held up the train."

The two robbers hurried to the wagon and fled into the darkness while LaGrange and Edgar rushed back to the train.

LaGrange, Edgar, and Pacey, who had regained consciousness, worked feverishly with axes to cut away the tender beam that pinned Masters's legs. It took an hour to cut him free. During the first thirty minutes, he was in shock, but he did not lose consciousness or hope, until finally he began to beg for a pistol to end his misery. By the time they cut Masters free, he was dead. While the men worked to free Masters, a brakeman ran to a nearby farmhouse and borrowed a horse. He galloped the 4 miles to Burbank and telegraphed the sheriff in Los Angeles. A posse was quickly formed and hurried to the scene. They recovered the bodies, took them to Los Angeles, and delivered them to the undertaking rooms of Garrett and Samson. The coroner conducted an inquest the following day, and then the remains of Masters were sent to Sacramento for burial by his brother while the remains of Daly were shipped to San Francisco for burial by his mother.

At the scene the posse found distinctive wagon tracks, as it appeared the wheels did not track perfectly, but again a heavy rain fell and obliterated the trail. They found along the way tags from the bags of stolen coins, but when, after 7 miles, the wagon tracks and trail of tags played out near Lankershim, they gave up the pursuit. The lawmen set up roadblocks on the road to Los Angeles, but the deputies missed the robbers. The Southern Pacific Railroad increased its reward from $1,000 for the two men to the same amount for each man in addition to Wells, Fargo & Company's standard $300 for each man, and the state added another $300 for each robber, bringing the total rewards to $1,600 each.

After a week John Johnson, Alva's older brother, informed on his brother and said he also suspected "Kid" Thompson and George Smith of the train robberies. He said he saw his brother and Smith with "$20 gold pieces similar to those taken in the robberies." Now with someone to focus on, the investigation turned to making a case, and the detectives learned that a man in Glendale had seen Thompson board the train the night of the robbery. They checked Johnson's wagon and found the wheels did not track perfectly because of a worn axle. The description of Johnson matched the taller robber, and the second man was about the same size as Thompson or George Smith.

Will Smith, Southern Pacific Railroad's detective, and Wells, Fargo & Co.'s detective John N. Thacker questioned Johnson and found him suspiciously agitated, but he made no admissions. They learned that Thompson had disappeared just after the robbery, and no one knew where he had gone. On March 26, Johnson and George Smith were arrested. The detectives felt certain that Johnson would weaken and "peach" on Thompson, but instead he hired two top attorneys and continued to insist on his innocence. The preliminary hearing was held on March 31, and the evidence was so weak that Justice Bartholomew refused to hold them. The search for Thompson continued, but by June attention turned to three other men, who were arrested and tried that month. Again the evidence was weak, and a verdict of not guilty was returned after only a few minutes deliberation.

In October detective Will Smith learned that Thompson was in Phoenix and went there to question him. After several interrogations the "Kid" gave him no useful information, so Smith returned to Los Angeles.

A few days later Southern Pacific Railroad's agent in Arizona, Billy Breakenridge, interviewed Charles Etzler, who was then working at the Baker ranch on Tonto Creek. Etzler disclosed that in September he had met Thompson, whom he had known in prison, while Etzler and another man were tramping on a train in California. Thompson told Etzler about the train robberies and said that he and Johnson were responsible. They went to the Johnson ranch where Thompson told Johnson that he was broke and demanded money. Johnson had buried the Mexican coins so that Thompson would not sell them to the Chinese in Los Angeles or give them away, and now Thompson wanted his share. Johnson told him to go to Tempe, Arizona, and he would send it along in a crate labeled "survey instruments." Johnson also gave him some money and a pistol. When Thompson and Etzler went to Tempe and found the package waiting, Thompson immediately sold his Mexican coins, valued at $600, to the Chinese at Phoenix for $240. Thompson was joined by a young man named H. L. Tupper, who was nicknamed "Colonel," and about this time Etzler decided to part company with the train robber and his new partner. The informant said that he knew where Johnson had hidden his share of the Mexican silver and was willing to show the lawmen where it was buried. Will Smith hurried to Phoenix, took Etzler back to Johnson's ranch and found the plunder, which proved him a reliable informant.

Detective Smith returned to Phoenix, and on October 14 he and Breakenridge went to a nearby ranch where Thompson was reportedly working. Thompson was away, so the lawmen left word with the rancher that they wanted to talk with Thompson again. Smith was certain that, since Thompson had been cooperative earlier, he would come to them not suspecting he would be arrested, but when Thompson was told that the lawmen wanted to talk with him again, he saddled his horse and fled with "Colonel" Tupper. Smith, with a deputy U.S. marshal, went in pursuit but lost the trail. Breakenridge knew that Thompson was familiar with the area around Agua Caliente on the Gila River and had many friends there, so he told Maricopa County Deputy Billy Moore to watch for the fugitive. On November 6 Moore heard that two men matching the description of Thompson and Tupper had been seen at Reno Pass heading for Tonto Basin, so he gathered a posse of four men and went in pursuit. They overtook the fugitives and called for their surrender when Tupper said, "Well, you've got the drop on us."

However, rather than surrendering, they began firing their six-shooters at the posse and fled into a box canyon. The gunfight continued until dark when the lawmen called for their surrender once more, and Thompson answered, "We'll die first."

There was no escape from the canyon as the lawmen waited at the mouth for the men to make their break, and at daybreak the posse began firing at the natural rock barricade behind which the boys were hiding. Finally the two youngsters realized escape was impossible and continuing the fight was futile, so they shouted, "We've had enough!"

They walked out with their hands raised, and the lawmen found behind the rocks two .44 caliber six-shooters and 200 rounds of ammunition, besides dozens of casings from the rounds they had fired. They were searched and had only a little more than a dollar between them. The two prisoners were brought in to Phoenix and turned over to Breakenridge, who took Thompson to Los Angeles when the fugitive waived extradition. When pressured to talk about the robberies, he told the district attorney, "I am not going to put a rope about my neck with my own hands. If you gentlemen will assure me of a life sentence I'll tell you all I know, otherwise I'll stand trial and let you prove me guilty."

With Thompson in custody, Johnson was rearrested and at his preliminary hearing was held over for trial on November 1. When Thompson joined him in jail on November 8, Johnson began to weaken and, to avoid a death sentence, confessed and agreed to testify against Thompson.

Thompson's trial for train wrecking commenced on May 1, 1895, with Johnson, Etzler, and George Smith testifying against him. The defendant took the stand and said he was innocent of the charge and had not even been in California at the time. The trial lasted five days, and after twenty hours of deliberation, Thompson was found guilty on May 8. A week later Judge B. N. Smith sentenced him to hang. An appeal to the Supreme Court was filed and Thompson was held in the jail, rather than the prison, pending a decision. The lower court's decision was upheld in February 1896. Thompson was taken to San Quentin, but a second appeal was filed on new grounds, which stayed the execution. The high court granted a new trial, which began on April 13, 1897. He was again convicted of train wrecking, but this time he was given a life sentence and sent to Folsom prison, so he would have no contact with Johnson, who was serving a life sentence at San Quentin.

Johnson tried to escape on July 19, 1900, and his partner in the attempted breakout was killed. Johnson was quickly captured and returned to prison, where he remained until October 20, 1907, when he was paroled. Three years later he was granted a full pardon. Thompson was paroled on December 14, 1909, but violated the terms of his release and was returned to prison for a year before being paroled again. The "Kid" had been so thoroughly institutionalized that he could not make it on the outside, so in 1921 he voluntarily returned to San Quentin. He was released after only three months. Four years later, while still on parole, he died at the age of fifty-four.

CHAPTER NINE

BLACKSTONE SWITCH

In 1835 and 1837 the Five Civilized Tribes signed treaties reserving a large tract of land in what would become western Oklahoma, but then was named the Indian Territory. The treaties left large tracts of land "unassigned." These eastern regions were united with the Indian Territory to become the Oklahoma Territory on May 2, 1890. The U.S. Congress granted statehood on November 16, 1907. The Oklahoma Territory experienced its first train robbery at Vinita in 1882, but, in comparison to many western regions, Oklahoma seemed almost exempt from that line of work. Outside Oklahoma there were repeated attempts at robbing trains, but it would be seven years before another train would be robbed in the territory—at Pryor Creek. However, train robberies in Oklahoma quickly grew to epidemic proportions over the next five years with seven trains being robbed before November 1894. It was in that month, on November 13, that a gang of five men robbed the Katy No. 2.

The Missouri, Kansas and Texas Extension Railway, dubbed the MKT or Katy, was incorporated in 1865 from the earlier Union Pacific Railway Company (not related to the later Union Pacific Railroad) and the following year began planning its connection to the railroads of Texas by laying its tracks through the Oklahoma Territory. Texas and its railroads at that time were isolated from the rest of the country. The MKT was not chartered in Texas but nevertheless managed to lay its tracks into that state, reaching a point near present-day Denison in 1872. The company continued to expand its trackage and rolling stock until, by November 1894, it was operating 133 engines and 163 cars. The MKT was determined to open up the eastern markets to Texas and provide eastern manufacturers with a new, readily available market for their goods.

Nathaniel "Texas Jack" Reed, a hard case with a long criminal record, lived in Oklahoma in 1894. He had been born in Madison County, Arkansas, on March 23, 1862. He lost his father, a Union soldier who was killed in combat on November 16, 1863, and thereafter was shuffled between family members until he turned twenty-one and headed west. Reed was considered a small man at a time when men were much smaller than today's average, and throughout his lifetime wore his hair long in the manner of Indian scouts. He found work in Idaho, Wyoming, Texas, Colorado, and Oklahoma, where he worked at the Tarry ranch under the supervision of a foreman named Coffey.

Since Reed was always game, he was enlisted by Coffey for a train-robbing affair, and in the summer of 1885, according to Reed, was introduced to the trade when they robbed a train at La Junta, Colorado. Reed claimed his part in the affair was to stand on the platform at the door to the passenger cars, kick the door, holler loudly, and fire his pistol in the air to keep the passengers from interfering. For this work he received $6,000. He said that afterward he adopted that line of work and could no longer be satisfied toiling from sunup to sundown for a few dollars. Reed, like all western bad men, tended to embellish a story, but it seems likely that over the next nine years he robbed at least two banks, two stagecoaches, and one train and also captured a large bullion shipment in California.

Reed was living near Muskogee, Oklahoma, when he recruited black freedmen Buz Luckey and William "Will" Smith, and a full-blooded Cherokee named Tom Root, who was quite large and exceptionally strong. Reed had been busy gathering intelligence on treasure shipments and finally learned from his agent in Dallas that a large shipment was going to be carried on the northbound Katy No. 2 on November 13, 1894. He chose Blackstone Switch at Wybark as the site for the robbery, and on November 12 took his crew to that location to stage a practice robbery. The plan was for Reed to throw the switch just as the train approached, sending it onto a sidetrack, and Reed would then dynamite the doors to the express car. Root was assigned to enter the express car, break open the strong boxes, and secure the gold. Smith was assigned to capture the engineer and fireman, and Luckey was to stay with the horses.

When the Katy No. 2 approached on the day following the dry run, Reed threw the switch, but engineer Joseph Hotchkiss was watching the track closely and saw the signal light change from green to red. The alert engineer set the brake, opened the sand valves, and pulled the bell cord, and the bell signaled to the messengers in the express car that the train was being robbed. The train stopped short of the siding, so Reed, Root, and Smith ran toward the train yelling and shooting, with Luckey far behind slowly bringing up the horses. The actions of the robbers had the effect of scaring the engineer so completely that he jumped from the train and hid in a small ravine, with his fireman close on his heels. Thus, when Smith got to the engine, there was no one to capture.

The railroad had its share of agents in Dallas as well, and they had sent word to the trainmen that there might be an attempt to rob the train, so the treasure had been pulled from that run and sent on a later train. The express car on the Katy No. 2 had been filled with armed messengers, who included James F. "Bud" Ledbetter, Paden Tolbert, Sid Johnson, Frank Jones, and possibly as many as three others. Once the robbers got to the express car, Reed ordered the messengers to get out, not realizing there were more than a few hapless agents aboard, but the messengers refused. Reed and Root then moved to cover behind trees and began shooting into the car. To their surprise the guards returned fire, and the exchange was quite lively for nearly an hour. Finally Reed threw a bundle of dynamite at the car and blew off one end, and then stationed Root to guard the gaping hole so that the guards could not exit.

Reed next, with false whiskers in place to disguise his identity, went into the passenger cars and began taking up a collection. He produced a large sack and required one of the passengers, a young boy, to carry the sack while he held a revolver in each hand. He ordered the men to put their valuables in the sack as they passed and went through the first car, the second, and finally the third. He excused the poor and the women from making a deposit but managed to gather in $460, eight watches, and three pistols from the men.

Reed returned to the express car and signaled to Root with a whoop, which was returned with a turkey gobble. Reed, to his surprise, found the doors to the express car had been opened and several men were standing about. Undoubtedly his thoughts were on the treasure that he believed was aboard when he saw a figure with a revolver in his hand in the darkened area between the cars. Reed dodged the first shot at his head, but the man lowered his aim and fired again. The ball entered Reed's left hip and exited through the back of the right thigh. Shooting continued without further effect.

When it was quiet, Reed signaled to Root with a whistle, and the big man came quickly. When he learned Reed had been shot, he lifted him up onto his shoulder and, still holding his bag of loot, carried him to Luckey and the horses. He put Reed in the saddle as Smith joined them, and the four men rode off quickly.

The robbers had not gone one-half mile when Reed had to stop for a few moments. Root struck a match and examined the discharge from Reed's wounds, then announced that the bullet must have missed the bowels and intestines, as there was blood but not bile coming from the wound. About every half mile Reed had to stop again, each time halting a bit longer than the time previous. After they had gone a little more than 2 miles, he could not continue. Making him a bed of blankets under a rock overhang, each man took $15 and a watch and left the rest of the loot in the sack for Reed to use as a pillow. They promised to return the following day to bury their partner. The three men returned the next day bringing Nancy Chisolm along to prepare the body for burial, but when they arrived, they found Reed weak but alive. Chisolm rinsed and dressed the wound, gave him water, and the following day returned with food. Later they brought soap to clean and treat the wound and turpentine to kill the pain. After five days Reed warned Root and Chisolm that he had seen five separate posses pass by and ordered them to leave and not return again.

On the evening of the seventh day, a man stumbled upon Reed in his hiding place, but Reed insisted that he had been hunting and had taken a chill and was going to move on soon. He assured the stranger that there was no need for his concern and shooed him on his way. As soon as the man left, Reed took up his bedroll and sack of loot and, using his rifle as a crutch, hobbled 2 miles through heavy brush. Reed came to a fence and there built a fire and lay down to sleep. In the morning he found he had stopped near a farmhouse and saw a black man chasing after a mule. When Reed asked for breakfast, the man's wife gave him coffee and cornbread. When, however, Reed asked if he could stay, the farmer suspected he was one of the train robbers and asked him to go. Reed managed to walk only 300 yards before he hid in a briar patch to sleep. He was awakened at midday by a posse, which loudly searched the farmhouse and surrounding pastures, and threatened the farmer and his wife.

Reed stayed in the brush until 5:00 P.M. and then started preparations to cross the river when a party of men came upon him, asked directions, and then eyed him suspiciously. They went on after he claimed he had been hunting squirrels and showed the bloody sack, which contained his loot, satisfying their curiosity. The wounded robber waded the river and made his way to the home of James Dyer, a man who had been working closely with lawmen in the territory but would later be implicated in the robbery. Reed stayed there safely until late November when he went on the home of Tom Root's sister, Mrs. Dick Reynolds, whose husband was then in jail for a petty robbery.

Soon after the train robbery, the American Express Company posted a reward of $250 for the arrest and conviction of each train robber. U.S. Marshal George Crump sent a large party of deputies into the Indian Territory and S. Morton Rutherford sent another force of deputies into the Creek Nation. One of the posses burned the canebrakes in the Verdigris bottoms and, upon finding Reed's burned saddle, threatened to burn the crops. This had been authorized by "hanging" Judge Isaac Parker if the local residents did not turn over the thief, but they would not disclose his whereabouts. Reed was warned of the efforts being made for his capture, and it was decided to get him out of the territory. On December 9 he arrived in Seneca, Missouri, where Bill Lawrence cared for him. In February 1895 Reed had recovered sufficiently to travel alone and went on to his brother's home in Madison County, Arkansas.

Deputy U.S. Marshal Newton LaForce and his posse were engaged in a relentless pursuit of the train robbers. Will Smith had left the country and would not be heard of again, but they had found the trail of Reed and, though they lost him, it led them onto the tracks of Root and Luckey.

On the foggy morning of December 5, 1894, LaForce, with an Indian police officer named Birchfield and a force of six men, surrounded the home of Root near Broken Arrow, 15 miles south of Tulsa. After watching for a short while and seeing no sign of life at the cabin, LaForce and Birchfield decided to examine the haystacks 200 yards distant. As the officers moved about, the dogs at the cabin were alerted and began barking, alarming Luckey, Root, and Root's wife who were asleep in a haystack. The two fugitives jumped from the hay and, faintly seeing two figures in the dense fog, began firing at them. The two deputies returned fire even while LaForce was commanding the fugitives to surrender. When the shooting started, the six posse men, who had remained on watch at the cabin, rushed to assist LaForce and were shooting in the direction of the fugitives. LaForce was shot in the back and died instantly while Root was shot through the thigh. Root and

Luckey escaped, but Luckey was captured at Muskogee a week before Christmas, taken to Fort Smith, and indicted for the murder of LaForce. Root remained at large, but refused to leave the vicinity of his home and wife.

By April 1895 Reed had considered his situation and wrote to Judge Parker, agreeing to turn himself in if he could be granted immunity for himself and Tom Root. He named the other robbers, since Luckey was already in jail for murder and Smith was out of the country, and he implicated James Dyer as the brains of the Blackstone Switch operation.

Word of his surrender and terms were sent throughout the region by telegraph, and on August 13 Tom Root surrendered to Deputy Jim Pettigrew at Muskogee. Judge Parker promised immunity for both men if they testified against Dyer in the train robbery case, but after Root was arrested, he learned that he was also charged in the murder of LaForce. Root then agreed to testify against Luckey at his murder trial, which began at the August term. The evidence showed that LaForce had writs for the arrest of both men, so Luckey was easily convicted of first-degree murder. Judge Parker said in sentencing him, "You, by the evidence, are a man of blood. You belong to the banditti, to the band of men who robbed and plundered peaceable citizens, express cars and passengers on railroad trains. The officers were seeking your arrest for robbery. You did not permit them to make their mission known before you fired on them and killed Marshal LaForce. You are now about to be sentenced to death for this wicked murder." He then sentenced Luckey to hang on October 20.

J. Warren Reed was Luckey's defense attorney, but no relation to Nathaniel "Texas Jack" Reed, and he filed for and was granted a stay of execution while Luckey's case was being appealed. The conviction was reversed by the U.S. Supreme Court on January 27, 1896, which set aside the death sentence and ordered a new trial. At the spring term of court, lawyer Reed presented a map of the location of the killing of LaForce and, by careful placement of each person involved, showed that neither Luckey nor Root could have fired the fatal shot and showed that LaForce had been killed by a stray bullet from one of his own deputies. Luckey was acquitted of the murder charge but was immediately charged with the Blackstone Switch train robbery and tried in the circuit court. He was convicted of obstructing a railroad and three counts of robbery for which he was sentenced to twenty, five, five, and five years respectively to be served consecutively, making thirty-five years in all.

He was delivered to the prison at Colombus, Ohio, under a contract with the federal government to house federal prisoners. He arrived on May 20, 1897, where he was registered as prisoner No. 29390. His earliest release date was recorded as June 27, 1919, but on April 7, 1901, at the age of thirty-one, Luckey died and was buried in Colombus's Greenlawn Cemetery.

The trial of James Dyer, Nathaniel Reed, and Tom Root began September 5 when Reed and Root testified that Dyer had shown them a telegram stating that a shipment of over $10,000 would be on the northbound Katy No. 2. They testified that Dyer laid out the plan for taking the treasure, but said that Dyer claimed to be ill and that was the reason he was not in on the robbery that night. The plan called for them to meet at Vann's Ford the following night and divide the loot into five equal shares. Based upon the testimony of Reed and Root and 106 other witnesses, Dyer was convicted of the train robbery and sentenced to fifteen years in prison, but an appeal was immediately filed. In consideration of his testimony against Dyer and Luckey, Root was released but the following year was killed in a gunfight at Concharty.

Dyer won a new trial on his appeal, and the case was delayed for a year and a half while each side tried to bolster its evidence. He was finally arraigned on March 22, 1898, and put on trial for the train robbery. With Root dead, the only witnesses against Dyer were now Reed, Root's widow, and a carpenter named L. M. Best. Best was easily discredited on cross-examination by lawyer Reed, who had been retained by Dyer after his success in the Luckey murder trial. Widow Root's testimony seemed coached, probably by her husband before his death, so Nathaniel Reed's testimony stood alone against the testimony of a large number of respectable citizens of Wagoner. The witnesses for the defense proved that Dyer had run a horse race at that place the day of the robbery and had returned home so late he could not have been involved. Dyer also showed that he had been assisting U.S. Marshal J. Shelby Williams in tracking and capturing bad men in the territory for some years. The marshal produced more than 200 letters providing information to the lawman, including several letters regarding the Blackstone Switch train robbery, the names of the robbers, and where they could be arrested. Dyer was acquitted of the charge and set free.

Although Reed had been promised immunity by Judge Parker, he was convicted of train robbery at his September 1895 trial and sentenced to serve five years in prison. However, Reed served less than a year of his sentence when Judge Parker, before his death in November 1896, kept his word and paroled Reed on November 18, 1896. Reed had finally had enough of the outlaw trail and, upon his release, became an evangelist. He traveled about giving sermons on the rewards of a respectable, law-abiding life. In his later years he produced several pamphlets on his thrilling life as an outlaw, stressing the downside of a life of crime as a lesson to those who might stray from the straight and narrow path, and sold his pamphlets to supplement his old-age assistance checks. On January 7, 1950, at the age of eighty-seven, Reed died a peaceful death in bed at his home in Tulsa, Oklahoma, and was buried at St. Paul, Arkansas.

CHAPTER TEN

COW CREEK CANYON

Cow Creek Canyon was a lonely place in 1895, 30 miles south of Roseburg and 8 miles south of Riddles in Douglas County, Oregon. The mountain passes in the canyon were of such a peculiar formation, with many sharp curves, that trains had to travel at a slow rate of speed, never exceeding 26 miles an hour in the dry season and much slower in the wet season.

On Monday evening, July 1, 1895, there was a bright moon, but the canyon was pitch black because the moonlight was blocked by the precipitous mountain on one side of the canyon, which was covered with heavy timber that made it seem all the more dark and gloomy. At 10:15 P.M. the Southern Pacific's northbound train No. 15, the California Express, was bound for Portland when it entered Cow Creek Canyon. The only light for the train was the powerful headlamp, and to the sides the dim lights from inside the cars. Fireman Everett L. Gray was stoking the engine to get up a good head of steam before they reached the steep grade ahead, and he was being assisted by a hobo who had hitched a ride and agreed to work rather than be put off. Suddenly there was an explosion under the engine, and engineer J. B. Waite, thinking it was a warning torpedo set by a section crew making repairs ahead, immediately applied the brakes.

This first explosion blew away the flanges of the pony trucks, disabling the engine. As the train came to a halt, there was an explosion at the front of the train and another in the rear, but neither of these explosions caused any damage to the train or tracks. As the train sat idling and the trainmen were contemplating their next move, three masked men approached the train. The leader, at gunpoint, took the engineer, fireman, and hobo prisoner.

R. E. Smith, an insurance salesman, and two friends stuck their heads out of the smoker window to see what was happening, but retreated quickly when a robber pointed a gun at them. The conductor ran forward to determine the problem and nearly ran into one of the robbers, who fired a warning shot and ordered, "Get inside and stay there." He went to the Pullman car from where he could see one of the robbers patrolling the bank above the cars, so he hid.

The lead robber, the only one to make personal contact with the trainmen, took Waite, Gray, and the hobo to the express car and demanded that expressman Ralph M. Donahue open the doors. The expressman had the presence of mind, at the first alarm, to remove the treasure from the local express box, hide it under some goods, and relock the box, so when the order came to open the door, he surrendered without resistance. As all the hostages piled in, the robber ordered them to keep their hands up. He then told Donahue to open the safes, and the local box was unlocked. The robber found nothing he wanted and ordered the through safe opened, but Donahue said he did not have the combination. The robber said, "I believe you are lying, but I'll come back and blow it up with dynamite," then drew a bead on Donahue's head and said, "I'll give you just five minutes to open that safe."

The plucky expressman replied, "Well, you are simply wasting time. I can't and won't open it. The combination is not given me, just because of such occurrences as this. So if you are going to shoot if I don't open it, you are wasting time to wait five minutes."

The robber replied, "You're hot stuff, ain't you!"

Postal Clerk Hermann.

Wood cut of postal clerk Hermann

They remained in the express car a little more than ten minutes before the robbers took the four hostages to the mail car, where mail clerk C. A. Hermann opened up only after being threatened with dynamiting the car. The robber needed assistance getting into the mail car, and this was supplied by his hostages. Once inside, his first demand was for the registered mail. Hermann later said he had little mail when they left the station at Glendale. When he discovered the train was being robbed, he had spread the local packages and registered pouches about the coach in various hiding places. As a result, when required, he produced only three of the registered pouches, and this seemed to be all he had. The robber made Hermann cut them open at the point of his pistol, then take out the packages and throw them on the floor at the robber's feet. Hermann complied, and the robber tore open the packages, taking out the money but throwing away all the other contents. He next asked for the local packages, and Hermann replied, "It's Sunday, you know, and I haven't many. They are scattered in those pouches."

The robber then went through the few pouches indicated and took out only five packages, leaving unmolested forty-five others that were well hidden. "What kind of ticker do you have?" the robber asked.

Hermann said, "I have an old one given me by my father some years ago."

The robber told him to keep it and then ordered him to join the party. Hermann pleaded that he had not slept for many hours, and he looked very tired. He asked to be allowed to shut the door and sleep, and he was permitted to do so.

The robber-leader took the hostages to the first passenger car, which was a day coach. Donahue walked ahead with a lantern, followed by the hobo carrying an empty sack supplied by the robber. The party went through the coaches from front to back, first the two day coaches, then two tourist sleepers, a smoker, and two Pullman sleepers. As they proceeded through, the party picked up the two brakemen and the porter named "Old Squab," making eight hostages in all, but left J. G. Ryan, the black buffet man, at his station.

In each car the robber announced, "Remain perfectly quiet, gentlemen. If I am hurt, you'll all go too. I have a dozen men outside loaded down with dynamite, and you'd better not try to be funny," and sometimes remarked also, "I'll give you a lift if any harm comes to me."

To emphasize their resolve, two robbers walked along each side of the train at the same pace as the interior party, firing their pistols into the air periodically and exploding a stick of dynamite every few minutes. At each seat in the forward passenger cars, the plunder was gathered by Old Squab and put into the sack carried by the hobo. In the smoker they encountered a man about twenty-three years old. When told to "dig," he began to cry.

Express Messenger Ralph M. Donahue.

Wood cut of express messenger Ralph M. Donahue

"What's the matter?" the robber asked, feigning sympathy.

"That's all the money I've got," the youth sobbed as he handed over a few dollars.

"Is that so?" replied the robber with a simulated whimper. "That's too bad," and then pretended to burst into tears. Still, he had Old Squab take the money and put it in the sack.

When he came to Klamath County's Sheriff A. A. Fitch, who was transporting a prisoner, the lawman said he had no money, only a revolver, and the robber took his blue steel B caliber Colt revolver with black handles.

When the party reached the sleepers, the robber asked at each berth, "Man or lady?" Old Squab would tell him, and the robber, who had taken an immediate liking to him, never checked. He only robbed the men who were in the lower berths and took nothing from the women or from any man who appeared to be a laborer.

He asked one man, "Got any money?"

The man replied, "A little."

The robber said, "Well, keep it. You look like a hard-working man and I guess you need it."

He told a pair of passengers, "Oh, you're broke, I suppose? And you too, poor fellow. Dig up. Got a watch? Let's see it."

When the second man produced an old watch, the robber said he could not use it in his business and threw it on the floor. The robber was somewhat disgusted at the poverty of the passengers, whom he said were "silver men." He told them he was a "gold bug" and told them to dig for their gold, but most of the passengers had suspected what was happening before his arrival and hastened to hide their valuables before he appeared. The process of going through the coaches took more than fifteen minutes, and near the end of the ordeal, the robber seemed anxious and on several occasions asked his hostages to tell him the time.

Once the party of hostages and the robber-leader stepped onto the rear platform of the last car, the trainmen were ordered to the front of the train. Old Squab was left on the platform and called to the robber, "Let me know when you're through, sir, and I'll tell the conductor."

The robber replied, laughing, "Get in that car, you black rascal, or I'll blow your head off. I'll let you know in plenty of time to start the train."

Seeing that the robbing was done and the robber was in a good mood, the engineer expressed concern for his engine and said he wanted to check it, but the robber said, "Oh, damn your engine! You stay where you are."

As they moved forward, the expressman and fireman were directed into the express car and ordered to close the door, and then the engineer was allowed to go to his engine.

Once inside the express car, Donahue gave a shotgun he had hidden in there to Gray and grabbed his revolver to await the return of the robber to blow up the through safe, as he had promised to do. However, when the hostage party got to the engine, the robber-leader just continued walking until he came upon his two partners and then turned and fired three shots, putting out the engine's headlamp. The three men walked into the brush and disappeared into the darkness. By the time Donahue and Gray got the door of the express car opened, they were unable to get a clean shot at the robbers, but the robbers kept shooting until they were entirely out of sight. Their take was soon calculated at about $1,000 from the mails and $520.70 from the passengers, but nothing had been taken from the express car. The damage to the train required the engine to uncouple, go ahead to a siding where it could turn around, and drive the train into Roseburg backwards, which delayed the report of the robbery another three hours.

The superintendent of the Southern Pacific Railroad telegraphed to the sheriff of Josephine County to go in pursuit of the robbers and to spare neither effort nor expense. The following day a circular was issued by Oregon's line manager, R. Koehler, in which he described the inside man as "5 feet 11 inches in height, native born American . . . light complexion, light moustache, hair cut close, light gray or blue eyes . . . weight about 170, high cheek bones, upper jaw protrudes over the lower one, bridge of nose swollen as though poisoned with poison oak, [wearing] blue overalls with jumper, light checkered vest or checkered cotton shirt, heavy stodgy shoes about number 8. The Southern Pacific Company will pay a reward of two thousand dollars ($2000) for the arrest and conviction of each of the robbers."

It was also noted by some witnesses that the leader of the robber gang seemed to be familiar with trains, was about thirty years old, and had a rich baritone voice. Koehler later amended his reward offer to say that it was being jointly offered by the railroad and Wells, Fargo & Company and included the standing reward of $300 per robber offered by Wells, Fargo & Company.

In response to the robbery and the rewards, there were several posses in the field, some on the way to the scene while others spread into the country trying to intercept the robbers on their most likely routes of escape. Sheriff C. F. Cathcart and Riddles' constable George Quine rushed to the scene of the robbery with a small posse. Quine was an amateur detective, so when he began to find evidence, he documented it carefully. There was a campfire near the tracks where the robbers had apparently waited for some time for the train's arrival, and there they found distinctive boot prints, one with two rows of tacks in the heels. The foot tracks were followed to the place where the robbers mounted.

The posse then followed the trail of horse tracks, and one of the horse's shoes had quite a peculiar design. The trail led them to a more permanent camp. Here they matched the horse tracks and boot prints and found the masks, which had been made from a sugar sack, and a rag from a flour sack used to bind a wound. They learned that the robbers had used giant powder sticks $3/4$ inch in diameter, which were not used by the railroad but by miners, so it was believed the men had brought them some distance to do the work and were probably miners or acquainted with mining.

On July 2 Stilly Riddle, who lived near the town of Riddles, went into Roseburg after he heard all the details of the train robbery, especially the description of the men. He reported that there were three men who had been working for some time at Nichols Station, which was 13 miles south of Riddles, and at least the lead robber matched the description of one of those men. Two of the men had been seen near the site of the robbery on the day before the robbery, and they were heading toward the tracks, but after the robbery they had disappeared from the area. One, according to Stilly, always wore a white hat with a buckskin band, just like the one described as worn by the robber who went through the train cars. He said he knew the men as Jim Poole and John Case. It happened that the lawmen were familiar with these two men, who had been sent to prison in 1890 on separate charges, met there, and became friends. Poole had been released in 1892 and Case the following year. They had settled near Canyonville, living off and on with Poole's father, Napoleon. With the focus on named suspects, the search centered on Napoleon Poole's house, and his sons, Jim and Albert, were arrested within a few days. Napoleon let the lawmen search, and they found sacking and string that matched that in the robber's camp. Furthermore, both Jim and Albert Poole's boots matched exactly the boot prints with the peculiar double tack design on the heels. Case was arrested later that day, and he would be identified as the man who had gone through the coaches, as his mask of light cloth had revealed his face to many of his victims.

At their preliminary hearing the three men were held to answer to the U.S. grand jury, indicted, and taken to Portland to await trial at the fall session. Though they were questioned closely, they would not confess nor "peach" on each other. The trial of the Poole brothers and Case commenced in the United States District Court in mid-December on a charge of robbing the U.S. mail. It lasted five days, one to seat the jury and four days to take testimony. On Christmas Eve at 3:00 P.M., after one hour of deliberation, the jury returned a verdict of guilty for Jim Poole and John Case, but not guilty for Albert Poole. Everyone on the defense side was astonished with the verdict against Jim Poole, but not the verdict against Case, and even the judge said, "I am frank to say that I am not entirely satisfied with the verdict."

Defense attorneys W. W. Cardwell and Albert Abraham filed a motion for a new trial. After months of contemplation Judge Bellinger set aside the verdicts and granted the motion. The prisoners had remained in the jail pending the Judge's decision, and he ordered them released without bond and set the trial for June 28. Case made his way to Tacoma, Washington, and on May 23, 1897 was shot dead while trying to rob a streetcar. The robber was positively identified as Case by several men who knew him from prison in Oregon. Plus he had used the same Colt revolver when arrested for train robbery. When his photograph arrived from Roseburg the identification was perfected. Case had been the mastermind of the Cow Creek train robbery, and Poole may never have gone astray without his influence. After Case's death the indictment against Poole was dismissed.

CHAPTER ELEVEN

PEACH SPRINGS, ARIZONA

leming "Jim" Parker and Jim "Harry" Williams, alias Charles or
John Creighton (sometimes spelled Crayton), were cowboys working for the Arizona Cattle Company near Flagstaff, Arizona, and
living at Abe Thompson's cabin. Williams was a cowboy and claimed to
have been in Buffalo Bill's Wild West Show. Parker was a "horse breaker"
and was exceptionally good at his trade, finishing well in Prescott's 1895
bronco-busting tournament. They enjoyed the thrilling life of the cowboy, but there was never enough money to finance their sprees, so they
decided to try what others had done successfully to enhance their for-
tunes—rob a train.

In December 1896 they burglarized the nearby cabins of two other
cowboys and took two Winchester rifles, food, and several Selsor shirts,
which they cut up for masks. Parker and Williams enlisted the help of
cowboys Abe Thompson and Lovell "Love" or "Kid" Marvin (sometimes
spelled Martin). They had Marvin go to Peach Springs to collect some
money owed him, but it was not there. When he returned, Parker,
Williams, and Thompson told Marvin they were going to hold up a train,
but they did not want him or Thompson to take part except to help them
get away, and Marvin agreed. Parker then sent Marvin and Thompson

into Peach Springs for ammunition and dynamite, but Marvin went to Kingman and bought the .40-60 ammunition at Watkins Drug Store and the .44 and .45 ammunition at Taggart's Store while Thompson got two sticks of dynamite from Mickey Nelson's barn in Peach Springs. Parker and Williams had one of the stolen Winchester rifles, and Marvin and Thompson each gave up his six-shooter to the two aspiring train robbers.

Parker chose February 8 as the date for their venture and selected a particular Atlantic & Pacific train as their target. On the day before the robbery, Marvin got two fresh horses for him and Thompson to ride. He and Thompson were to go into Peach Springs and make themselves conspicuous, and then they would be "robbed" of their fresh horses while returning to their cabin, at which time they would receive their share of the plunder. Parker and Williams would flee north across the Colorado River into Nevada and camp at a spring familiar to all four men while Marvin and Thompson were to return to town and turn loose the spent horses, then follow the robbers into Nevada in ten or twelve days. The four men rode to within 7 miles of Peach Springs before they separated.

On the bone-chilling evening of February 8, 1897, Parker and Williams, carefully masked in black, went to the rock cut 8 miles east of Peach Springs near mile post 457. At 7:15 P.M. they captured night watchman Edward Allen. Williams kept guard over Allen while Parker marched up and down the tracks to keep warm and watch for the passenger train. Twice freight trains came through, but finally at 8:50 P.M. the passenger train appeared. Parker forced the watchman to flag the train, and the engineer signaled with two blasts of his whistle to acknowledge the sign for danger and then stopped the train. Allen was standing beside the tracks when Engineer Bill Daze asked him to explain the problem ahead, but Daze got no answer. The engineer then asked if there was some obstruction ahead, but Allen still stood silent. At that moment a masked man entered the cab of Engine No. 85 and took charge at gunpoint. The two robbers took the fireman, engineer, and watchman to the rear of the express car where they had the fireman

Lovell "Love" or "Kid" Marvin
SHARLOT HALL MUSEUM, PRESCOTT, ARIZONA

uncouple the remainder of train No. 1. When the fireman seemed to be stalling, Williams said, "If you don't hurry up I will shoot your heels off," so he quickly completed the uncoupling.

Parker took the trainmen back to the engine while Williams remained on the platform at the rear of the express car to guard against interference from anyone from the passenger cars, and Williams fired five shots along the side of the train to keep the passengers inside. Parker, once back in the engine cab, ordered Daze to pull the engine forward to Nelson's Siding 2 miles west and then fired one shot into the air, apparently a signal so Williams would know he was still in control of the engine as it moved forward.

While the express cars were being uncoupled from the passenger cars, the express messenger, who was alerted by the unscheduled stop and several gunshots, armed himself with a .45 caliber revolver and, with his assistant, jumped from the opposite side of the express car. They ran toward the rear of the train, but when they came abreast of the rear platform of their car, they came face to face with Williams, who was armed with a Winchester rifle, a revolver, and several sticks of dynamite. The messenger did not hesitate but fired two shots in rapid succession. The first ball entered Williams's breast just above his heart and passed entirely through his body. As the robber slumped to the ground, dying from the mortal wound, the second ball struck him in the left eye and exited at the back of his head, killing him instantly. The train was then under way, so, when the two expressmen hesitated for a moment, they missed their chance to board the rear platform of the mail car and were left behind with the passenger cars.

The engine, tender, express, and mail car pulled ahead 2 miles to Nelson's Siding and stopped, and Parker had the engineer block the engine. Parker took watchman Allen to the mail and express cars and found the express unguarded. Parker went into the mail car and, with mail clerk A. S. Grant waved aside at gunpoint, went through the registered mail and selected nine packages that looked as if they contained valuables. Parker then ordered Daze to back the engine halfway toward the passenger cars where he fired four shots into the air as a signal, and looked north of the tracks as if expecting someone. When there was no reply to his signal and no one came, the engineer was ordered to drive the engine back to Nelson's Siding where Parker said, "Get out of here as soon as God will let you." He added, "I am short two men," but he made no effort to find them and then walked off into the brush.

Daze backed the engine to the passenger cars, coupled them to the mail car, and continued on to the next destination where the robbery was reported. The most substantial clue was the dead bandit lying on the rear platform of the mail car, who was described as about 147 pounds and forty years old. He was believed to be a former employee of the Arizona Cattle Company working as a cowboy near Flagstaff, and it was thought the other robber was an acquaintance from the same place.

In Peach Springs Thompson and Marvin made certain they were noticed throughout the day. After sunset Thompson went to bed while Marvin muffled up his feet with saddle blankets from Nelson's barn and went up on the hill to watch. When no one came, Marvin went back into town and prepared to go to bed, but Thompson said, "Let's go down to the train," and when they got outside Thompson said that "the men made a failure of it and Williams has been killed." They returned to Thompson's cabin to wait. It was not long before Abe Thompson and Lovell "Love" Marvin were under arrest. Marvin was not a hard case and quickly weakened and confessed, and on March 22 had the confession written out and signed. Marvin turned state's evidence and, in consideration of his testimony, was released.

Sheriff George C. Ruffner of Yavapai County, with Deputies Martin Buglin, Ed Riley, and Tom Rogers, was soon on the track of Parker, and Indian trailers were employed. The pursuit was mostly on foot as Parker had intentionally chosen the most rugged terrain in that part of the country for his escape. On Sunday afternoon Ruffner, Buglin, and Riley fell back on their trail to butcher a beef while Rogers went ahead with the Indians. Rogers's party stumbled upon Parker, took him prisoner, and set up camp to await the arrival of the sheriff with meat for the evening meal. Parker suddenly seized upon a moment of laxity, leaped forward, and grabbed a Winchester rifle, which he pointed at the deputy. Rogers retreated rapidly, and when Parker fired one shot, the Indians scattered into the brush and circled around to look for the sheriff.

The next morning Ruffner, Buglin, and Riley started up Diamond Creek searching for some sign of Parker. The party had not gone far when they saw the fugitive coming down the canyon making his way toward the Grand Canyon. They set up a crossfire ambush and waited. When Parker came abreast of Ruffner, he called out, "Hands up!"

Parker turned toward the sound, rifle at the ready, when the two deputies at his back repeated the same command. Parker looked over his shoulder and realized he was covered from both sides. Seeing resistance futile and probably fatal, he complied with the order and surrendered his Winchester. The following day Parker arrived at Prescott and was lodged in jail. On February 24 Parker was taken before Justice J. M. W. Moore for his preliminary hearing and held for trial.

On Sunday, May 9, 1897, seven weeks before his trial, Parker escaped from the county jail with forger L. C. Miller and Cornelia Asarta, a Mexican charged with an attempted murder at Crown King. Prescott's *Miner* reported:

DESPERATE JAIL BREAK THIS AFTERNOON . . . Lee Norris, who comes to Meador's Assistance, Shot Down by Parker with a Charge from a Shot Gun. One of the most daring jail breaks ever attempted by desperate men was successfully made at 1 o'clock this afternoon from the county jail. It was accomplished by the probable fatal wounding of Lee Norris, assistant district attorney of the county, and brother of T. G. Norris. . . . After mounting they rode down the alley, south, between Marina and Cortez streets to Carleton near Judge E. W. Wells' residence where they rode west to Cortez street going south on that street.

The fugitives were well armed and well mounted and had no trouble making a clean getaway.

Lee Norris's wounds were not considered dangerous at first, as the shotgun was loaded with birdshot instead of buckshot. Norris was reported as resting easy, and his physicians had great hopes for his recovery. It soon became apparent, however, that Norris's condition would not stabilize. The evening of the escape, Norris developed alarming symptoms when "he commenced having hemorrhages. At times he seemed to rally sufficiently to inspire hope among friends that he might recover, when he would be attacked with sinking spells, and hope gave way to fear. His condition was such for hours, that hope alternated with fear with those who were tenderly caring for him until dark, when the physician pronounced his case hopeless, and he died just about midnight."

Norris seemed to know immediately that his was a mortal wound, and he told this to friends and doctors, giving instructions for the disposition of his remains. The charge against the fugitives was now murder and rewards were offered accordingly. The governor issued a Proclamation of Reward in the amount of $500 each for Parker and Miller and $250 for Asarta. The county would add to those rewards, and later Wells, Fargo & Company would offer an additional $1,000 for Parker.

Over the next several weeks lawmen and Indian trackers followed various trails, investigated sightings, and even had several encounters with the fugitives, but the fugitives remained free. On Tuesday, May 18, L. C. Miller was captured at Jerome. Miller was at once taken in a private conveyance from town as he was afraid of being lynched. Although his crime, forgery, was a small one, his association with the murder was enough to hang him, so he implored to be taken some place further from the scene of the crime. He was taken to Flagstaff by two Coconino County deputy sheriffs.

On Wednesday, May 26, just at daybreak, Parker was captured about 80 miles north of Flagstaff by S. S. Preston and ten Navajo Indians. Preston was engaged in merchandising in company with Hugh Campbell at Willow Springs. On Monday Parker stopped at their place for dinner and was recognized by them. An Indian courier was immediately dispatched to Flagstaff with the information. After Parker left, Preston secured the services of ten Navajo Indians, who were not only expert trackers but brave men as well.

They started on the trail, following it during Monday afternoon and all day Tuesday. Toward nightfall on Tuesday, the Indians told Preston that they were close and that Parker had gone into camp. The posse proceeded cautiously until they located Parker's camp, surrounded it, and remained on guard all night. Just after daybreak the following morning, about 4:45 A.M., they closed in on their game. One of the

Indians fired off his gun to awaken Parker, who jumped to his feet with his Winchester in his hands, but found eleven deadly weapons pointed at him. The fugitive was taken completely by surprise, and Preston demanded that he lay down his gun, throw up his hands, and advance six paces. Seeing that, once again, resistance was useless, Parker obeyed the mandate, contrary to all expectations as it was thought that he would fight to the death. The Indians closed in on him and bound his hands securely. The march to Flagstaff was commenced. With two of the escapees in jail, attention turned to the third fugitive—Cornelia Asarta, but he was never found. It was thought, from all the circumstances of the escape, that he died in the wilderness from a serious wound, an infection, starvation, or exposure.

While Parker awaited his trial for murder, Thompson was tried as an accessory to the train robbery, convicted, and on June 28 received a sentence of five and one-half years to be served in the Territorial Prison at Yuma. Parker and Miller filed motions for separate trials on the murder charge and also for a change of venue, but they were only granted separate trials. Miller, who had not fired a gun during the escape, was nevertheless convicted and sentenced to life in prison. He joined Thompson at the Territorial Prison near Yuma on Sunday, July 4, 1897. Parker was convicted of murder in the first degree and sentenced to be hanged on August 14, but various legal motions and appeals had to be disposed of before the sentence could be carried out. After nearly a year of appeals and motions, the date for the execution was set for June 10, 1898.

On Wednesday, June 8, the day that work commenced on the 18-foot-high enclosure surrounding the gallows, the *Miner* reported that while "In the Scaffold's Shadow" Parker experienced a change of heart and decided to join the church. Father Quetu baptized Parker into the Catholic Church on Thursday, and that evening the prisoner prepared for his death. For the first time since being returned to Prescott's jail, he asked for whiskey to stimulate him, which he drank freely but not to a point of intoxication. He finally fell asleep at 4:00 A.M. but was awake at

Hanging of Parker

SHARLOT HALL MUSEUM, PRESCOTT, ARIZONA

an early hour and ate a hearty breakfast. At 10:00 A.M. on Friday, June 10, Sheriff Ruffner read the death warrant to Parker in his cell, and at 10:25 they began the march to the scaffold. The sheriff had hold of Parker's left arm while Deputy Jeff Davis was on his right. Father Quetu and Undersheriff J. P. Dillon, Deputy Pete Boscha, and ex-Deputy Johnny Munds followed. In addition to the sheriff and his force of deputies, who assisted him, the execution was witnessed by Sheriff Ralph M. Cameron of Coconino County; ex-Sheriffs James R. Lowry and William Mulvenon, a deputy U.S marshal, and Prescott's chief of police.

As Parker emerged from the gloom of the jail into the bright sunshine of an unclouded Arizona sky, his gaze rested on the instrument erected for his death, and he was visibly affected and faltered for an instant. Quickly gathering his composure as they were about to lead him up the stairs of the scaffold, he said, "Hold on boys, I want to look at this thing; I never looked at one before."

Sheriff Ruffner permitted him to go under the scaffold and examine it. He spent several minutes, seeming to be especially interested in the release mechanism for the trapdoor. During his examination he made several remarks to the sheriff, but these were not recorded. After finishing his inspection, the prisoner ascended with a steady gait and stepped heavily upon the trapdoor, as if to try its strength, and said, "I will set my feet right on these two nails."

Parker took off his slippers and threw them carelessly on the floor of the scaffold. At this moment, seeing J. D. Moore among the spectators, he saluted him with a smile, saying, "Hello, Jack! How are they breaking?"

While the condemned man was speaking, Sheriff Ruffner commenced buckling the straps around his legs, and the prisoner said, "Take your time, George; there is no use in putting them on; I am not going to straddle out; you needn't worry."

After Parker's arms and legs had been pinioned, Undersheriff Dillon told him that if he had anything to say he could do so, and the prisoner said: "I have not much to say. I claim that I am getting something that ain't due me, but I guess every man who is about to be hanged says the same thing, so that don't cut no figure; whenever the people says I must go, I am one who can go, and make no kick."

The black cap was then drawn down over his face when he said, "Hold on, I want to shake hands with the boys."

The cap was removed and he shook hands with all those on the scaffold, saying that he had no ill feelings toward anyone. After shaking hands with everyone, he motioned to jailer Morgan and shook hands with him a second time, holding his hand for a few seconds, remarking, "It's all off; tell the boys [those in the jail] that I died game and like a man."

The black cap was again drawn over his face and Undersheriff Dillon was adjusting the rope while Sheriff Ruffner had his hand on the lever of the trapdoor, preparing to spring it, when Parker said, "Don't get excited; George, you put her on."

Undersheriff Dillon had the rope already adjusted properly, but Sheriff Ruffner gave it a pull and at the same moment sprung the trap. Parker shot downward 6 feet, the whole thing being done so quickly that the spectators could scarcely watch the movements. The trap was sprung at exactly 10:31 A.M. after which there were several convulsive twitches of the legs, and these were the only motions perceptible.

Dr. E. W. Dutcher and Dr. J. R. Walls were the official physicians in attendance, and they timed Parker's pulse. At the expiration of ten minutes and fifty-four seconds, life was declared extinct and the body was cut down. An examination showed that Parker's neck had been broken in the fall. When the black cap was removed the features of the deceased appeared perfectly natural, with the exception of the open eyelids and a slightly drawn appearance to his mouth. The body was at once removed to undertaker Logan's establishment where it was viewed by a number of people during the afternoon. Parker was buried at the expense of the county in Potter's Field at 4:00 P.M.

CHAPTER TWELVE

THE WILD TRAIN-ROBBING BUNCH

The Wild Bunch was aptly named. They were certainly wild by any standard, but they were also more a bunch than a gang. On any outing the participants could include any number of different men, and this may have been intentional as lawmen often had to guess which men had participated in any particular robbery. At times there were 100 to 150 desperate men hiding at Hole in the Wall, but the "train robbing syndicate" consisted of fewer than a dozen of these desperados. Like many aspiring train-robbing gangs, members of the Wild Bunch syndicate started out in other criminal endeavors before graduating to robbing trains, and they learned their trade on the job. The first train-robbing effort, a crime of compulsion and opportunity, did not even include the leader.

On July 14, 1898, a Southern Pacific train was robbed near Humboldt, Nevada. The robbers were described as "two white men and a Negro" but later the modus operandi suggested it was members of the Wild Bunch, identified as Harry Alonzo "Sundance Kid" Longabaugh, Harvey "Kid Curry" Logan, and "Flat Nose" George Curry. They got more than $20,000, made a clean getaway, and returned to Hole in the Wall, where they shared their experiences with leader Robert Leroy "Butch

Cassidy" Parker. Cassidy decided to try his hand at robbing trains and adopted the unique feature for their *modus operandi* of using explosives to open the safes. They never bothered to first determine if the safes could be opened by the messenger and always used far too much dynamite for the job. However, Cassidy was very thoughtful in his planning of their getaway. He knew that posses would be on their trail quickly, so he developed a system of horse relays so his men would always have fresh horses for their getaway. For days before a robbery, he would scout the region for good horseflesh, building a string that was very fast over short distances. These animals would be ridden to the place of the robbery. Next he would get as many strings of horses as needed and position them along the escape route, and these would be horses bred for endurance. He would see that all the horses were pampered for days before they took the road by being fed grain, exercised daily, and rested.

On June 2, 1899, eleven months after the train robbery in Nevada, the Union Pacific Overland flyer train No. 1, which traveled in two sections each with its own engine, was stopped at milepost 609 by two men waving lanterns. There was a small wooden bridge ahead and engineer W. R. Jones thought it might have washed out. An engineer could not jeopardize his train by ignoring an emergency signal, so Jones brought his train, the first section, to a halt 1 mile west of Wilcox, Wyoming, at 2:09 A.M.

When the two men boarded the engine, Jones saw they were masked and armed. One of them ordered Jones and the fireman to pull the train forward across the bridge and stop again. When the train was in position, dynamite was exploded, destroying the bridge, so that no one from the second section could interfere when that train arrived. Four more robbers went to work on the express car and, without demanding entrance, dynamited the rear end. The four men did not bother to ask messenger Ernest C. Woodcock if he could open the safe but instead used another charge of dynamite to blow it open. The contents were quickly removed, and the robbers disappeared into the darkness. Later their trail revealed that they had horses tied a short distance

*Portrait of the Wild Bunch, left to right: Harry Longabaugh (The
Sundance Kid), William Carver, Ben Kilpatrick (The Tall Texan),
Harvey Logan (Kid Curry), and Robert Leroy Parker (Butch Cassidy)*
DENVER PUBLIC LIBRARY, WESTERN HISTORY COLLECTION, Z-49

away and had ridden north toward Casper. The trainmen could not identify any of the robbers, so the lawmen who investigated could only guess
that they were members of the Wild Bunch and supposed the robbers
included Cassidy, Logan, and Curry, but the other three robbers
remained unknown. It was reported that the men got very little, as there
was not much in the safe and a substantial part of the currency was
destroyed in the blast. Rewards of $3,000 per man ensured that there
would be many large posses in the field, and it was estimated that nearly
400 men participated in the pursuit at different times and places.

On Saturday afternoon a Union Pacific special train arrived at Casper with Converse County's Sheriff Josiah Hazen, fresh horses, and men. A local rancher, Al Hudspeth, reported that three men were camped at Casper Creek 6 miles northwest of town and had run him off at gunpoint when he stopped to visit. When he described the men, the lawmen knew they were Logan, Curry, and William Ellsworth "Elza" Lay. Inquiries were made and it was determined that the three men had stopped in Casper to buy supplies. Hazen called for reinforcements and the CY outfit provided ten men to supplement Hazen's posse of ten men.

The posse took the field Monday and from Casper Creek followed the trail to within 5 miles of a horse ranch at Salt Creek. They had proceeded only a few hundred yards past that point when Curry shot and killed posse member Tom McDonald. Oscar Heistant, sheriff of Natrona County, had his horse shot from under him, so he was sent afoot to the nearest ranch with orders to bring back more men. The three fugitives continued a running gun battle throughout the day.

On Tuesday Hazen and Dr. J. F. Leeper came to a draw and dismounted to look for a trail. Just as Hazen signaled he had found the tracks, Logan rose up from behind a boulder, took careful aim, and shot the sheriff in the stomach. The three fugitives kept up the fire for a short time, but when the rest of the posse came up, they mounted and fled. Hazen was taken back to Casper and then by special train to Douglas, where he died at 5:00 A.M. The killing of Hazen outraged Wyoming's citizens. A hundred trackers were dispatched to look for tracks, the U.S. marshal organized a posse of fifteen hand-picked deputies, bloodhounds were put on the scent, the state militia was mobilized, and more than a hundred men volunteered for posse service. Even with all the lawmen's effort and large rewards the three train robbers managed to elude capture and fled the region.

The Wild Bunch syndicate took two months off, waiting for interest in the huge rewards to wane. Finally on August 29, 1900, they were ready to rob another train. One of the robbers slipped aboard the "blind baggage" of Union Pacific's train No. 3 second section as it pulled out of

This train car exploded during a robbery by the Wild Bunch.
DENVER PUBLIC LIBRARY, WESTERN HISTORY COLLECTION, X-22288

Tipton, Wyoming, which is located midway between Rawlins and Rock Springs in Sweetwater County. He climbed over the tender and took the engineer and fireman hostage at gunpoint. When the train was 2¹⁄₂ miles west of Tipton, he ordered the train stopped. Three other robbers appeared from the shadows and began shooting their pistols along the sides of the passenger cars to prevent any interference. When they felt secure, the robbers went to the express car and forced their way in by threatening to dynamite the car. E. C. Woodcock, the same messenger they had robbed at Wilcox, opened the door and gave no resistance. As soon as they were inside they placed a large charge of Kepauno Chemical Company giant powder, a 40 percent explosive from the Ashburn Works in Missouri, on the through safe and blew it apart, along with most of the express car. The amount taken was later disputed, with the Pacific

Express Company reporting a loss of $50.40, but Woodcock said he was carrying $55,000, and Cassidy later claimed they had taken $45,000; but there was also $3,000 worth of damage done to the express car. The gang buried the treasure, believing for some reason that it could be easily traced to them and, as a group, rode to Huntington, Nevada. This time, the railroad offered rewards of $1,000 for each man and the express company added another $1,000 per man, bringing the total to $8,000. But the robbers again eluded lawmen.

One month after robbing the train near Tipton, the men who had fled into Nevada robbed the bank at Winnemucca, Nevada, to finance their next train-robbing endeavor. Then, once again, the Wild Bunch laid low until interest in them cooled.

The Tipton robbery convinced the railroad that it needed to do something unique to stop the robberies of its trains in Wyoming. Recognizing the efficient getaway method of relays of fresh horses, the railroad started dispatching special horse-car trains to the robbery scene as soon as a robbery was reported. An elite posse with fresh horses delivered by special train could arrive in a short time and take up the pursuit, in contrast to arriving later with spent mounts and then following a cold trail.

Aware of the Union Pacific's new practice in Wyoming, the gang chose Montana and the Great Northern Railway in June 1901. Cassidy, Logan, and Ben Kilpatrick, along with Kilpatrick's companion Laura Bullion, went to Wagner, Montana, where they planned to rob a train. They recruited Camilla "Deaf Charley" Hanks, a local train robber, for the fourth robber. (Bullion was an accessory, but it is unclear what her role was.) Wagner, Montana, was to be Cassidy's final robbery, so he was being exceptionally cautious. He had plans to flee to South America and needed a big haul. The plan was to rendezvous with Longabaugh, who was already aboard a ship bound for Argentina in the company of Etta Place.

On July 3, 1901, Kilpatrick boarded as a passenger at Malta, Montana, while Logan slipped onto the "blind baggage." When the train neared Exeter Switch, 3 miles east of Wagner, Logan climbed over the tender and captured engineer Tom Jones and his fireman at gunpoint. The other two robbers, Cassidy and Hanks, were waiting on the tracks and waved a flag to signal the place to stop the train. The two outside robbers fired their pistols along the sides of the cars to keep the passengers from interfering, but several shots were too close and ricocheted into the cars, causing several minor wounds. The front of the train was uncoupled, and the engine, tender, and express cars were pulled ahead. The robbers broke into the express car and blew open the safe, which contained $40,000, mostly in bank notes sent to the Montana National Bank in Helena. The plunder was loaded onto horses, and the four robbers rode south across the Milk River and turned east.

After four days following the trail, lawmen said they believed that the fugitives were better mounted than any of the posses and were probably somewhere between the Missouri River and the Hole in the Wall. This area was sparsely settled and quite rough, and it was felt that any further pursuit was "virtually hopeless." Later the lawmen learned that the robbers stopped in Miles City and purchased four fresh horses, using stolen bank notes for the purchase. The Great Northern Express Company offered a $5,000 reward for their arrest and $500 for each conviction. Descriptions of three of the men were circulated:

One was height 5 feet 9 inches, weight about 175 pounds, blue eyes, had a projecting brow and about two weeks growth of sandy beard on chin, wore new tan shoes, black coat, corduroy trousers, and carried a silver plated, gold mounted Colt's revolver with a pearl handle. Second man: height 6 feet, weight 175 pounds, sandy complexion, blue eyes, not very large with slight cast in left eye, wore workingman's shoes, blue overalls over black suit of clothes, had a boot leg for cartridge pouch suspended from his neck. Third man resembled a half breed very strongly, had large dark eyes, smoothly shaven face, and a very prominent nose, features clear cut, weight about 180 pounds, slightly stooped in shoulders, but very square across shoulders, and wore a light slouch hat. All three men used very marked

Texas cowboy dialect, and two of them carried Winchester rifles, one of which was new. One had a carbine same pattern as the Winchesters. They rode away on black, white and buckskin horses respectively.

Cassidy was never captured. He booked passage to South America and, with Longabaugh and Etta Place, tried the honest life of a rancher. It was generally believed that he later returned to a life of crime and, with Longabaugh, was shot to death in a cantina. However, there later surfaced some evidence that both men returned to the States and lived out their lives in peace and freedom under aliases.

<> <> <>

The leader of the Wild Bunch syndicate was Robert Leroy "Butch Cassidy" Parker, his first recruit was Harry Alonzo "Sundance Kid" Longabaugh, and his right-hand man was William Ellsworth "Elza" Lay. Parker was born in Beaver, Utah, in 1866. He was still quite young when he left home after a minor skirmish with the law—more a misunder-standing than a crime. He soon met Mike Cassidy, and the two engaged in cattle rustling. In 1884 altered brands were discovered and the cattle traced back to Parker. He fled and, to ensure that his family would not be shamed by his criminal activities, he adopted the alias Butch Cassidy. He went to Telluride, Colorado, and tried to follow the honest path of a teamster, but he was too restless to settle down. After a few months he moved on to Wyoming. He befriended others interested in making quick, easy money, and in 1889 he led a small party to Telluride and robbed the San Miguel Bank.

Cassidy laid low for several years after the Colorado bank robbery, but in 1894 he was arrested for stealing horses, tried, convicted, and sen-tenced to prison at Laramie, Wyoming, for two years. He may have been innocent of the charge, but prison hardened him, taught him about crime, and convinced him he needed to form a gang. After his release in 1896, he met Harry Longabaugh, who became his first recruit. There seemed little reason to delay, so in early 1896 Cassidy, Longabaugh, and others robbed a bank in Utah and in August robbed another bank at Montpelier, Idaho. Then, in April 1897, Cassidy and Lay robbed the Pleasant Valley Coal Company mine payroll at Castle Gate, Utah. Perhaps Longabaugh shared his experiences with train robbery, since the next affair they planned was an assault on a train.

Harry "Sundance Kid" Longabaugh was jailed for horse theft in Sundance, Wyoming, which earned him his sobriquet. He served eighteen months and was released. He was soon jailed again for a minor robbery but escaped.

On November 27, 1892, the westbound Great Northern Railway train No. 23 left Minnesota headed for Butte, Montana. When the train was pulling out of the small station of Malta at 3:00 A.M. the following morning, three men swung aboard the "blind baggage" of the express car just behind the tender. They pulled up their masks and climbed over the tender, taking the engineer and fireman hostage at gunpoint, and demanded the engineer bring the engine to a halt.

The two trainmen were marched to the express car, used as a shield, and the robbers commanded messenger Jerry Hauert to open up while assuring him they meant him no harm. The messenger opened the door and let in the robbers, who then demanded he open both safes. Hauert opened the local safe, in which there was about $20, but convinced the men he could not open the through safe. They believed him and departed into the early morning darkness.

During the robbery the masks kept slipping and all the trainmen got a good look at each robber. They provided descriptions, and within a few days Bill Madden and Harry Bass were arrested at Alex Black's saloon in Malta. They confessed to the robbery and named twenty-four-year-old Longabaugh, the "Sundance Kid," as the third robber. Longabaugh had left the region and was never arrested for his part in the train robbery. On July 14, 1898, Longabaugh was near Humboldt, Nevada, with Harvey Logan and "Flat Nose" George Curry, when they robbed a Southern Pacific train of more than $20,000.

William Ellsworth "Elza" Lay began his criminal career in 1884. He participated in the Montpelier bank robbery and the Castle Gate payroll robbery before taking part in his first Wild Bunch train robbery at Wilcox, Wyoming. After the Wilcox affair, Lay, Cassidy, and Logan fled south through Arizona into New Mexico where they hid out at the WS Ranch, using aliases and working as cowboys. Lay met Sam Ketchum in New Mexico and on July 11, 1899, with Ketchum, Will Carver, and Bruce Weaver, held up a train near Folsom, New Mexico. Lay was arrested, convicted on October 10, 1899, and sentenced to life in prison.

Harvey "Kid Curry" Logan began his criminal career on December 27, 1894, when he shot and killed Pike Landusky in Montana and fled to the Hole in the Wall. He participated in a series of stagecoach and bank holdups and was a participant in the killing of Deputy Sheriff William Deane on April 3, 1897. He was arrested at Deadwood but escaped jail. Logan was with Longabaugh and Curry when they robbed the Southern Pacific train near Humboldt, Nevada, on July 14, 1898. He was also one of the men at the Wilcox train robbery.

On May 27, 1900, he killed Moab, Utah, Sheriff Jesse Tyler and his deputy, Sam Jenkins, to avenge the killing of George Curry. He participated in the Tipton train robbery with Longabaugh and Cassidy. He also participated in the train robbery at Wagner, Montana, with Cassidy, Kilpatrick, and Hanks. He fled to Texas and then to Tennessee where he wounded two officers in Knoxville and was jailed, but he escaped and participated in a train robbery at Parachute, Colorado, on July 7, 1903. Two days later he was so badly wounded by a posse that he killed himself. His brother, Lonny Logan, was never associated with any of the robberies, but when he visited an aunt in Missouri, Lonny was surrounded by a posse and killed in the shootout that followed.

"Flat Nose" George Curry, sometimes spelled Currie, went to the Hole in the Wall during its early days as a bandit's redoubt. He led a gang of rustlers but soon expanded his operations to include stagecoach holdups. On June 28, 1897, he was in a party of six who tried to rob a bank at Belle Fourche, South Dakota, but they were all captured and jailed. They escaped on December 4 and were at the Hole in the Wall shoot-out on December 15. He took part in the robbery of a Southern Pacific train near Humboldt, Nevada, on July 14, 1898, in company with Longabaugh and Logan.

Then, as a member of the Wild Bunch, he participated in the train robbery at Wilcox. When several members of the bunch fled south into New Mexico, he remained in the Utah and Wyoming area and returned to his rustling activities. He was caught in the act of altering brands on cattle and in the ensuing gun battle he was killed by Sheriff Jesse M. Tyler. Curry's body was taken to Chadron, photographed, and then buried. Curry was twenty-seven years old, 5 feet 10 inches tall, 175 pounds, light complected with brown eyes and dark hair. He had a prominent nose but with the bridge flattened, which accounted for his sobriquet.

Camilla "Deaf Charley" Hanks was wanted for rape and murder in New Mexico when he fled to Montana as a drover with a cattle herd. Hanks, under the alias Charley Jones, assisted in a train robbery at Graycliff, Montana, on August 25, 1893. The gang got $52 from the local safe and a small sum from two passengers. Hanks was arrested for a murder he had previously committed and was tried in Helena on January 10, 1894. Hanks was convicted of first-degree murder and sentenced to death, but, on December 22 of that year, his sentence was commuted to ten years. He was released from prison on April 30, 1901, in time to join the Wild Bunch by July 3 when they robbed the train at Wagner. Following that robbery he fled to San Antonio where lawmen tried to arrest him at his boarding house. He resisted arrest and was shot to death.

Ben "the Tall Texan" Kilpatrick had been a member of the Ketchum Gang in New Mexico, but by mid-1901 he was associating with the bunch. He participated in the train robbery at Wagner and then fled to St. Louis, Missouri. On November 8 he was captured, extradited to Montana, tried, convicted, and sentenced to serve twelve to fifteen years. He served his entire sentence, less good time, and was released on June 11, 1911. He partnered with an old cellmate, Ole Beck, and armed with a

Winchester rifle the two men tried to rob the Southern Pacific Express at Sanderson, Texas, on March 13, 1912. Messenger David A. Trousdale, a plucky new guard, crushed Kilpatrick's head with an ice mallet and then, taking the robber's rifle, killed Beck.

Laura Bullion was with Kilpatrick when he went to Brown's Hole, Colorado, in 1895. They later associated with the bunch. She played a supporting role in the train robbery at Wagner and accompanied Kilpatrick to St. Louis, where she was arrested in his company. In Montana she was convicted as an accessory to the robbery and on December 13 was sentenced to serve five years in prison. She remained faithful to Kilpatrick until his death and then disappeared from the record.

CHAPTER THIRTEEN

THE KETCHUM GANG

W ho was "Black Jack?" There was a William "Black Jack"
Christian active in the Southwest just before the turn of the
century who had recently been killed by a posse when the
Ketchum brothers appeared on the scene. One story suggests that
Thomas Ketchum, who was a 6-foot-2-inch Texan, dark complected with
dark hair and eyes, fled into Arizona after he and his brother Sam robbed
a train and was hiding out near Bisbee when a saloon patron mentioned
that Thomas resembled "Black Jack" Christian, who was also a tall, dark-
complected Texan. After hearing of his look-alike's daring exploits, he
adopted the sobriquet "Black Jack." Another explanation is that a deputy
sheriff mistakenly thought Thomas might be "Black Jack" Christian and
announced his theory to the newspapers. When he learned his error, he
tried to correct the misidentification, but Tom Ketchum's nickname
stuck. There was even some talk that Sam Ketchum might have been the
real "Black Jack," but Sam was light complected with freckles and sandy
hair, hardly the type to be "Black Jack." Thomas Ketchum always denied
that he was "Black Jack" or that he ever used that nickname.

Thomas Ketchum was involved in a number of train robberies
during his brief criminal career, but it is the last train robbery, a failed

attempt, for which he is best remembered. On August 16, 1899, Ketchum tried to rob a train single-handedly and was badly wounded and arrested. While in prison his wounded arm became infected and was amputated. He was convicted of the same offense twice, and became the only man in the West to be sentenced to death for a crime other than first-degree murder. But it was his execution—the most bungled execution on record—that earned him a place of prominence in the annals of the western frontier.

<> <> <>

In 1849 Peter Ketchum led two wagon trains into Texas where the Ketchum families established several cattle ranches. Peter's oldest son, Green, came from Illinois with his wife, Temperance, and one-year-old daughter Elizabeth, and they settled in Caldwell County. Temperance gave birth to Green Jr. in 1853, and the following year Samuel was born on January 4, 1854. Nancy B. Ketchum was born six years later, just before the family moved to San Saba County, and on October 31, 1863, Thomas Edward Ketchum was born. When Green Sr. died in 1868, Green Jr. supported the family until his mother passed away in 1873.

Samuel had left home to work as a cowhand but was destitute when his sister Nancy took him in about 1880. Thomas remained with Green Jr. when he moved his family to Tom Green County in the early 1880s. During 1885 Samuel came and went for several months before Thomas joined him herding cattle. Thomas left because he had some minor skirmishes with the law during those early days, so when Green Jr. married the sheriff's daughter, he told Thomas to be out of the house for good when he returned from his honeymoon.

After Tom joined Sam, the two younger Ketchum boys worked on various ranches from Texas to Wyoming over the next five years, when they became close friends with William R. Carver and David Atkins. Carver had been born in Comanche County, Texas, in September 1868.

"Black Jack" Ketchum
WESTERN HISTORY COLLECTIONS, UNIVERSITY OF OKLAHOMA LIBRARIES

After his father abandoned them, his mother remarried and moved the family to Pipe Creek in Bandera County where Carver was introduced to the cowboy life by his uncle Dick. In early 1892 he married Viana Byler, but within a few months she became terminally ill and died in July. Although he had other relationships, he never married again.

Atkins was a native of Tom Green County and met the Ketchums when they moved there in the early 1880s. He married Saba Banner in 1894 and soon had a baby girl, but Atkins was not a good father or husband and abandoned his family.

On December 12, 1895, John N. "Jap" Powers was brutally murdered, shot in the back three times from ambush when he stepped into his horse pasture, with the *coup de grace* inflicted to his head from close range. Tom Ketchum, Atkins, and another man were eventually indicted, but they had already fled from Texas. The following year the sheriff of Tom Green County insisted that the three men were innocent and declared that he would not pursue them further as Power's wife and another man became the focus of his investigation. Meanwhile Carver and Atkins turned up in the Arizona Territory while the Ketchum brothers were working on the Bell ranch in the New Mexico Territory.

When Samuel had a dispute with the ranch foreman, the boys left but soon returned to steal supplies from the Bell storehouse. This was the first crime attributed to the Ketchum boys acting together, and it was followed quickly by a burglary of the post office and store at Liberty. One of the owners of the store, Levi Herzstein, and Merejildo Gallegos pursued the Ketchums and were shot to death. The Ketchums fled into the Arizona Territory to avoid a murder charge and joined Carver and Atkins in Graham County. Atkins left for a while but soon returned.

Tom Ketchum, Carver, and Atkins headed south to Lozier, Texas, a water stop on the Galveston, Harrisburg & San Antonio Railway. Just before 2:00 A.M. on May 14, 1897, Ketchum and Carver climbed over the tender, covered engineer George Freese and fireman James Bochat with pistols, and took control of the train. They stopped the engine at the next cut where Atkins had severed the telegraph wires and was waiting with their horses and explosives. The three men entered the express car, took agent W. H. Joyce prisoner, and blew open the way safe after two attempts failed. From the safe they took three sacks of plunder, which Wells, Fargo & Company would later value at $42,000. Several posses were soon in the field, but the three robbers managed to avoid them and made their way to Tom Green County, where they spent nearly all they had stolen in buying support to stay hidden.

When their money ran low, the boys decided they should rob another train, this time in New Mexico even though that territory had made train robbery a capital offense in 1887. Thomas was joined by brother Samuel while Carver and Atkins enlisted the help of a fifth man named Charles Collings, and the party of five made their way to the Twin Mountains bend between Folsom and Des Moines.

On September 3, 1897, they stopped the southbound No. 1 train of the Gulf, Colorado and Santa Fe Railway, and messenger Charles F. Drew was brutally assaulted by Samuel Ketchum. As in the previous robbery, it took three charges to blow the safe, in which they found less than $3,500 in cash, some assorted jewelry, and other small items. The gang hid for several days in Turkey Creek Canyon near Cimarron, New Mexico Territory, and then headed for the southeastern corner of Arizona Territory, where the gang then began planning its next robbery. One man was arrested and tried for the crime, giving his name as Bruce "Red" Weaver. There was, however, little evidence to tie him to the robbery, and he was acquitted.

Deputy U.S. marshals had not been able to find the robbers, but in late November 1897 they received word that a train would be robbed at Stein's Pass in early December. On December 9 Stein's post office was robbed by Atkins and Ed Cullen, but they got only $9 for their effort. The two men then joined Thomas Ketchum at the depot and searched the offices of the express company located at the Stein's Pass Station, where they found a little more than $2 and a Winchester .44. Ketchum and Carver took the horses 2 miles further west and built fires on both sides of the tracks at a point where there was a steep grade.

The westbound No. 20 train came along at 9:00 P.M., and the men who remained at the station forced station agent Charles St. John to show a red warning light to stop the train. They boarded the engine and captured the fireman and engineer Thomas W. North, whom they then forced to pull ahead to the fires. Once the train was in position, the robbers approached the express car, but messenger Charles Jennings and two guards began firing at them. Four robbers were wounded, Cullen was killed, and the gang was forced to flee, leaving Cullen's body behind. Three innocent men, all hard cases and criminals, were indicted, tried, and convicted of the post office robbery. Despite the later confessions of the Ketchums, they remained in prison until 1904.

The gang had made the robbery attempt at Stein's Pass because they were short of money. After the failed attempt, they were broke, so they were anxious to secure another large haul. They returned to familiar territory near Lozier, Texas, and this time chose for their work the Comstock Station on the Galveston, Harrisburg and San Antonio Railway, halfway between Langtry and Del Rio.

On April 28, 1898, at 11:30 P.M., the westbound No. 20 was leaving the station when two armed men, carefully masked, climbed over the tender and captured engineer Walter Jordan and his fireman. They ordered him to stop the train, and as soon as it came to a halt, two men appeared and uncoupled the passenger cars from the rear of the express car. They forced Jordan to take the engine, tender, and express car westward to Helmet before they stopped the train again and approached the express car. Messenger Richard Hayes was about to make a fight of it when a cartridge jammed his Winchester and he had to surrender. The robbers cleaned out the safe and then blew open the through safe by putting the local safe on top of the charge to direct the explosion. The empty safe was blown through the roof of the car, the through safe was emptied, and later the take from the two safes was estimated at $20,000. It was seven hours before a posse could take the field, and it returned to town empty-handed, with no further clues or tracks to follow.

The Ketchum Gang decided that on its next job it would try the same ruse it had used unsuccessfully at Stein's Pass by displaying a red light, a warning of danger that no engineer could ignore. They moved north to Mustang Creek, and on July 1, 1898, stopped the westbound Texas Pacific No. 3 train, threw a switch, and directed the train onto a siding. The passenger cars were uncoupled, and the engine, tender, and express car were pulled ahead some safe distance to prevent interference. They easily gained entrance to the express car and blew the safe with explosives. They took out an estimated $50,000, leaving behind a large number of $10 bills and assorted jewelry before they made their escape.

In the spring of 1899 the Ketchum brothers quarreled, and Sam Ketchum and Carver split from Thomas. Thomas went to Prescott, Arizona, where on July 2 he murdered two men. Meanwhile Sam Ketchum was forming his own gang, which included William E. "Elza" Lay (who had fled into New Mexico after robbing the train at Wilcox, Wyoming, with the Wild Bunch) and Bruce "Red" Weaver. The Ketchum Gang, before the split, had made plans for a repeat robbery at Twin Mountains, taking in the Colorado & Southern Railway, formerly the Gulf, Colorado and Santa Fe Railway.

Sam and his new partners in crime rendezvoused at Turkey Creek Canyon in May 1899 and began making preparations. Carver, in June, purchased two rifle scabbards, a .30-.40 carbine, and 1,000 rounds of ammunition made with the new smokeless powder developed in France. On July 7 the men bought supplies, delivered them to their hideout, and then started making their way toward Folsom.

On July 11, 1899, Sam Ketchum and Lay climbed aboard the "blind baggage" of southbound No. 1 while the engine was taking on water. The two men made their way over the tender and captured engineer J. A. Tubbs. Carver had gone ahead 2 miles and built fires on both sides of the tracks where there was an "S" curve, and the armed robbers had Tubbs stop the train at that point. Carver ordered express agent Hamil Scott to open the doors to the express car and fired several rounds, which caused the messenger to surrender without resistance. The first explosion did not open the safe, but the second was successful and peeled back the roof of the car as well. Conductor Frank Harrington and two passengers, who were deputy sheriffs but were unarmed, could do nothing but watch as the men packed a number of bundles onto their horses and rode off. Later U.S. Marshal Creighton M. Foraker would state they had gotten more than $30,000 in plunder.

The robbers split up, with Weaver given the responsibility of hiding the stolen loot and later recovering it for a division in Turkey Creek Canyon. Sam Ketchum, Carver, and Lay went into Cimarron, but they were too conspicuous and made no effort to cover their tracks when they left. They were seen entering Turkey Creek Canyon on July 15, and the following day a seven-man posse surrounded them in their camp. The lawmen discovered Lay near a pool of water 100 yards distant and shot him. As he lay wounded, he was shot a second time in the back. Sam Ketchum grabbed his rifle and got into the affray, but a bullet shattered his left arm and he fell, unable to continue shooting. Carver was above the camp, and his use of smokeless powder did not give away his location, so he was able to hold off the posse single-handedly. Edward J. Farr, sheriff of Huerfano County, Colorado, hid behind a tree for cover, but the .30-.40 rounds being fired by Carver had tremendous force and easily penetrated the tree, killing the lawman and filling the gaping wound with splinters. Posse man Henry Love was also badly wounded but lingered in terrible pain until he finally died on July 28.

The posse retreated, so Carver managed to get his two wounded partners into their saddles and lead them away. Sam Ketchum, however, was unable to continue, so he was left behind and captured. He was taken to Santa Fe where doctors tried to treat his wounds, but gangrene had set in. On July 24 he died from the infection.

Lay's wounds, though serious, only kept him down for a week. After he recovered, he made his way to Lusk's ranch where he was captured on August 16, while Carver made good his escape. Weaver had hid the loot as they agreed and later moved it near Alma, where he again buried it. Soon after securing the plunder for the second time, he was arrested, but Marshal Foraker released him on July 20, 1899, under the mistaken belief that he was innocent of the charge of train robbery because he had not been in Turkey Creek Canyon during the shootout.

Weaver recovered a part of the loot and lived well until April 8, 1901, when he was shot to death by William "Pad" Holomon in a gunfight, and most of the stolen money remained buried. Lay was tried in October 1899, and, under his alias William H. McGinnis, was convicted of second-degree murder and sentenced to life imprisonment. New Mexico's Governor Miguel Antonio Otero commuted the sentence to one to ten years, and Lay was released on Christmas Eve 1905. After

Weaver was arrested, he had told Lay where the stolen treasure was hidden. Although Lay lived well for years on the stolen money, by the time of his death from natural causes in 1934, he was destitute.

Tom Ketchum had heard nothing of the train robbery, the shootout, or the death of his brother since, in July 1899, he was on the trail heading toward New Mexico. He planned to reconcile with Sam and decided that it was time to execute their plans to repeat the robbery at Twin Mountains, not knowing it had already been done. When he was unable to find his brother, Carver, or any other gang member, Tom Ketchum decided to try the robbery alone. He abandoned his attempt on August 11, when he saw an armed guard in the express car at Wagon Mound, and then anxiously made his way to Folsom.

On August 16 at 10:20 P.M., Thomas Ketchum climbed aboard the "blind baggage" of the southbound No. 1 train when it stopped at Folsom to take on water. He captured engineer Joseph Kirchgrabber with his Winchester and had him stop the train at the bend 4 miles south of the station, 2 miles from the place Ketchum had tied his horse. The conductor was again Frank Harrington, who had been defenseless during the first robbery, but now had armed himself with a shotgun. In the express car was Charles Drew, the man badly beaten by Sam Ketchum in 1897, and in his care was over $5,000 in currency.

Ketchum ordered Drew out of the car and had him hold a lantern while fireman Tom Scanlon tried to unlock the couplings behind the express car. Instead the fireman cut the air hoses that locked the brakes on all the cars. Fred Bartlett, the mail clerk, stuck his head out to see what was happening. Ketchum, a remarkable marksman, fired a warning shot, but it ricocheted and struck Bartlett in the jaw, causing a serious but not fatal wound. Scanlon then said he had uncoupled the cars, but he had not, so Ketchum ordered the engineer to finish the task.

While Kirchgrabber struggled with the coupling, conductor Harrington opened the door to the first coach behind the express car, discharged his shotgun at Ketchum, and tore a gaping wound in the robber's right arm just above the elbow. Ketchum was going to shoot Harrington, but his shot went wild because he was struck by the buckshot first. Ketchum stumbled off into the darkness and sent a couple of shots toward the lantern, to discourage anyone from following, and managed to make it to his horse. However, he had already lost so much blood that he was too weak to mount or ride, so he lay down beside the tracks and waited to be arrested. The following day the posse arrived and easily captured Tom Ketchum.

Ketchum was arrested, indicted, tried for assault on a U.S. mail agent, and sentenced to a ten-year prison term. While he was being held at the prison, his wounded right arm became so infected that it had to be amputated. The following year Ketchum was tried again, this time for an "assault upon a railroad train with intent to commit a felony." This latter offense had been added to first-degree murder as a crime punishable by death in 1887, the only two capital offenses in the West. He was again convicted and this time became the first person sentenced to hang for assaulting a train.

As the date for the prisoner's execution approached, he was taken to Clayton in Union County and lodged in the jail. From his window he was able to see the carpenters constructing the gallows and the high board fence required by law, and he complimented them on their skill. He asked for female company as his one last request, but this was denied as there were no funds authorized to pay for a "lady of the town."

Father Dean from Trinidad stayed with the condemned man throughout his last night. In the morning the prisoner ate a hearty breakfast, washed himself, and then dressed in the new suit provided by the sheriff. After the death warrant was read, he seemed anxious to proceed, but it was still too early. At 11:30 A.M. he asked for music, and it was provided by a violinist and a guitarist as he ate his dinner. At 12:30 P.M. he named all those involved in his prosecution and promised that they were "marked for death" by members of his gang. At 1:15 P.M. Thomas Edward Ketchum began his march to the gallows accompanied by his priest, with Sheriff Salome Garcia on his right, Harry Lewis of Trinidad on his left, and a detective from Denver, Colorado, following.

The condemned man climbed the stairs with a firm step, his head down, and took his place upon the trapdoor. His arm and legs were pinioned, the noose adjusted, and the black cap pulled over his head. He had declined to make a speech, but when there was a brief delay he called out, "Let 'er go, boys!"

Governor Otero had sent a man to oversee the preparations and ensure that everything went smoothly. The drop was calculated at 5 feet 9 inches, a few inches longer than required for a man near 200 pounds, but at the last minute Sheriff Garcia, concerned the drop would not do the work, increased it to 7 feet. The rope had been carefully soaked and stretched with a heavy weight to remove elasticity, and then dried. The stretching made the rope, already thin for a hangman's noose, almost cordlike, and where fiber met fiber it was lubricated with soap to ensure the knot would slide easily. Another piece of rope was used to secure the drop, and the trapdoor was released by cutting this rope. When the moment arrived the sheriff cut the rope releasing the trapdoor with a single stroke, and the body shot downward. The rope cut through the neck, muscles, and spine, severing Ketchum's head from his body and both fell to the ground, with blood spurting from the torso's neck, the head in its black bag rolling about, and the bloody rope rebounding high into the air.

After photographers were done with their grisly work documenting one of the worst bungled executions in the West's history, the head and torso were collected by the undertaker and the head sewn on. Thomas Ketchum was buried in the town's cemetery the following day, the only man in the Old West to be legally executed for a crime other than first-degree murder.

CHAPTER FOURTEEN

COCHISE JUNCTION

O n September 11, 1899, constable Burt Alvord, his sometime deputies William F. "Bill" Downing and Billie Stiles, and Matt Burts met in the back room of Schweitzer's Saloon in Willcox, Arizona. They were engaged in a private poker game and had bribed the porter to periodically bring in a tray of drinks and take out an equal number of empty glasses, regardless of who was still present at the time. The four men then slipped out a window, snuck down the alley, and left town. Stiles and Burts collected the arms and dynamite hidden by Downing, mounted the horses he had hobbled and hidden outside of town, and then rode to Cochise Junction 10 miles southwest of town. Once they were on their way, Alvord and Downing returned to the back room of the saloon to ensure that the alibi for all four men would be airtight.

Alvord had been appointed the constable at Willcox because of his reputation in cleaning up rough towns. He had been raised on the streets of Tombstone just as the boomtown years were coming to an end in 1886. Although he had every opportunity to go bad, John Slaughter, sheriff of Cochise County between 1887 and 1890, hired Alvord as his deputy. Alvord, though a large and tough character, preferred using his six-shooters. He was not only a fast draw but also an exceptionally accurate marksman. He was hired to clean up the town of Pearce when it was

Albert Alvord

Billie Stiles

Matt Burts

William Downing

YUMA TERRITORIAL PRISON STATE PARK

out of control, and he was so successful that after he tamed that town, he was hired to perform the same service at Willcox. The constable had learned early on that the job of a lawman did not pay well, so he was open to suggestions for increasing his income. Still, he seemed to be doing an excellent job of taming Willcox, though several of his friends, particularly Bill Downing, were among the hard cases he was sworn to control.

Downing sometimes claimed to be the original Texas terror, Sam Bass, and knew so many intricate details of Bass's history that he could often convince the more gullible or less informed. However, Sam Bass was dead, and Downing was actually Frank Jackson, the only member of the Bass Gang to escape from Texas. He had not been heard of for two decades before he surfaced at Willcox using the Downing alias, and he became a friend and sometimes deputy or bodyguard for the town's constable.

Downing had some experience with train robbery while riding with Bass, and he knew how much plunder the express cars often carried, so it may have been at his suggestion that Alvord decided to become involved in a train robbery. Downing had learned also that there was considerable risk in being present at the scene of the robbery and made sure that neither he nor Alvord were put in jeopardy. His plan was that Matt Burts and Billie Stiles would rob the train, following his detailed instructions, while he and Alvord remained in Willcox to establish an alibi for all four men.

Stiles, another hard case, was born in Casa Grande, Arizona, but at an early age fled into Mexico to avoid arrest for murder. When he returned, he settled in the Willcox area, became a friend of Burt Alvord, and sometimes served as his deputy or bodyguard. Texas-born Matt Burts was the fourth member of the Alvord Gang, recruited for the specific purpose of robbing a train.

Stiles and Burts rode bareback to a spot $2^1/_2$ miles west of Cochise Junction and then walked east to the station to wait for the westbound Southern Pacific passenger train to arrive. Once the train stopped to take on water, the two masked men captured engineer C. E. Richardson and fireman Charles Bircher and had Richardson drive the train a mile westward, where they uncoupled the passenger cars from the rear of the express car.

The two robbers then forced Richardson to drive his engine, tender, and express car ahead another $1^1/_2$ miles westward and stop where they had left their horses. They directed the engineer and fireman, at gunpoint, to bang on the door of the express car and demand entrance. When the door was opened, express messenger Charles Adair surrendered without a fight. One robber covered all three trainmen while the second robber piled dynamite, which they had stolen from the Sot Brothers' store, around the safe, lit the fuse, and blew the door off the safe. He gathered up the contents, purported to be $30,000 in gold coins, many being newly minted, and packed them into several saddle bags.

The two men then quickly mounted and rode into the darkness of the Arizona desert. When they neared the town of Willcox, they released their horses into a herd grazing nearby and walked into town, then joined Alvord and Downing in the back room of Schweitzer's Saloon. The two robbers gave the loot to Alvord and he, in turn, gave each man a share of several hundred dollars. He later hid the rest to await a time when interest in the robbery subsided.

Once the robbers rode off, the engineer put his engine in reverse and backed up to the passenger cars, where the occupants had been unaware that they had been left behind. The fireman coupled the cars while the engineer tried to send a telegram, but he found the wires had been cut. A horse was found, and a rider was dispatched to Willcox to alert the lawmen stationed there. This delay provided time for Burts and Stiles to return to town and to the back room of Schweitzer's.

When the messenger arrived with news of the robbery, Alvord was duly outraged and immediately deputized Downing, leaving his poker partners Stiles and Burts in town to rest. Alvord and Downing rode to the scene of the robbery with a small posse. County Sheriff Scott White was also notified and put a posse in the field as well. It was still dark when Alvord's posse reached the scene of the crime, but they were soon on a trail although it was quickly lost among the tracks of the heavily traveled road toward Willcox.

Not only did the posse lose the trail, they entirely obliterated it until it was lost. There were no other clues, and the investigation had nearly ended within a month, until a newly minted $10 gold coin turned up in a saloon. Wells, Fargo & Company's detectives and Arizona Rangers were notified, and they traced the coin to Bill Downing, but he denied any knowledge of the coin and offered his alibi of the poker game to avoid suspicion. Ranger Bert Grover was not satisfied with Downing's explanation. He deduced that if Downing was involved then so were the other three men used as his alibi, but there was no evidence to implicate them. Since he could not proceed with arrests, he waited and watched for some opportunity.

There was clearly no progress in the investigation, so Alvord and his men became emboldened. The first robbery had worked perfectly, or so it seemed, so the men were anxious to try their hand again. This time Downing and Alvord recruited Bob Brown, George and Lewis Owens, Tomas "Bravo Juan" Yoas, and "Three Fingered" Jack Dunlap to do the work. They had three separate trains in mind but finally settled on the southbound between Benson and Nogales and chose the station at Fairbanks, a stopping place of some importance because it served as the depot for Tombstone. The greatest obstacle to a quick and lucrative robbery was express messenger Jeff Milton, a capable gunman who had served effectively in various posts as a lawman. Their concern with Milton was so great that they sent Stiles, an acquaintance of Milton, to ensure that the messenger would not be aboard by luring him away on some business proposition. Stiles seemed to have succeeded and the plan went forward, but the assigned messenger for the run took ill and Milton replaced him at the last minute.

The gang of five robbers rode to the Dragoons and camped on February 14, 1900. The next day they rode to Fairbanks and, playing the role of drunken cowboys on a lark, at gunpoint lined up all the employees and passengers they found at the station.

When the train rolled to a stop, Milton opened the door and began passing out the packages bound for Tombstone, when one of the robbers ordered him to hold up his hands. He looked out and found the five robbers standing behind the line of bystanders, using them as a shield. Although Milton's shotgun was close at hand and he picked it up, he could not fire for fear of killing the innocents, and his revolver was a distance away on his desk. When he did not comply, the robbers opened fire and several shots hit him in the left arm. The force of the bullets spun him around and he went down, so the robbers rushed the car. Milton quickly recovered, and using the sawed-off scattergun in his right hand, he fired point-blank into the body of the lead robber. Dunlap went down with eleven buckshot pellets in his side, and one pellet hit Yoas in his buttocks. Yoas fled and did not stop until he reached Mexico. Milton fell forward between two trunks, pulled the safe keys from his pocket, threw them into the pile of packages at the end of the car, ripped his shirt to make an impromptu tourniquet, and then passed out.

The robbers riddled the car with bullets before entering and once inside were about to shoot the unconscious Milton again, but engineer Avery pleaded that he was already dying and should be left alone. The robbers agreed not to waste a bullet, and one of the men searched Milton for his keys but, not finding them, made a quick search of the car before leaving empty-handed.

The robbers lifted Dunlap onto his horse, and the four men rode northeast toward Walnut Gulch. When they got to Buckshot Springs, Dunlap seemed about to die and was unable to ride further, so the three robbers abandoned their partner and rode off. The next day a posse led by deputy Sid Mullen found Dunlap lying in the road, still alive, though one kidney was shot to shreds, and he was taken to Tombstone. He lived for several days, and when it was certain he was about to die, he provided a detailed ante-mortem statement naming all the participants and their part in the robbery. He died of his wounds on February 22, 1900.

Yoas rode across the San Pedro River and into Mexico. He stopped at a ranch, but when the owner learned he had been involved in the shooting of Milton and thought the messenger dead, the Mexican barely escaped with his life. He continued on to Cananea where he sought medical treatment for the wound to his lower buttocks. The Mexican authorities had their own experiences with train robbers and wanted nothing to do with Yoas, and they were convinced the wound had come in the Fairbanks train robbery. The Mexican authorities arrested Yoas and delivered him to Sheriff White at the Mexican jail on February 23, when the prisoner waived extradition. Yoas was returned to the jail in

Tombstone where he received medical treatment, which may have been his motivation to return to American soil.

Following the statement by Dunlap, Brown was tracked down, arrested, and taken to Tombstone. The Owens boys were easily found at their ranch in the Sulphur Springs Valley and also arrested. Meanwhile a posse had gone to Willcox and arrested Alvord, Downing, and Stiles. Once all the suspected robbers were in jail, they were taken before Justice of the Peace A. T. Schuster and held to answer to the grand jury. On March 2, 1900, Alvord and Downing were taken before the U.S. commissioner and charged with the federal offense of obstructing the U.S. mails and then returned to jail. Stiles agreed to turn state's evidence and testify against his partners and confessed their involvement in the Cochise Junction train robbery, so he was released from custody on his promise to appear whenever called to court.

On April 7 at 3:00 P.M., Stiles went to the Tombstone jail and asked deputy George Bravin to allow him to talk with Alvord. Bravin allowed the meeting, but when he was taking Alvord back to his cell, Stiles suddenly pulled a revolver. During a struggle, Stiles shot Bravin in the leg. The cell doors were then opened and Yoas joined Alvord and Stiles in their escape, but Downing and the Owens boys refused to escape and remained in their cells. The three fugitives armed themselves with rifles and pistols from the sheriff's armory, stole several horses, and fled into the Dragoon Mountains. Rewards of $500 each were posted and generated a number of sightings all over the territory, but the fugitives remained at large until Stiles surrendered on July 1, 1900. Two days later Stiles was taken before U.S. Commissioner G. Davis and ordered held at the Territorial Prison near Yuma, where he was taken on July 6.

On October 10 the Owens brothers pled guilty and agreed to testify against the others in the Fairbanks robbery. Robert Brown was in court that day and was tried, convicted, and sentenced to ten years in prison while the Owens brothers, in consideration of their cooperation, were sentenced to only four years each. On December 6 Burts appeared in court, pled guilty, and was sentenced to serve five years in prison.

Downing was next to be tried on December 11, 1900, and he was charged with train robbery, which was a capital crime in Arizona. The jury acquitted him of the charge, so he was then charged with the federal crime of attempting to rob the U.S. mail and trial was set for the circuit court. There were some delays, but Downing was finally tried for the federal offense, found guilty, and sentenced to serve ten years. He arrived at the prison near Yuma on April 10, 1901.

Burts was pardoned on April 18, 1901, and was not heard of again until November 8, 1925, when he and J. W. Robinson killed each other in a dispute over water rights in San Bernardino County, California. The Owens brothers were released on February 15, 1903, and Brown was released in 1907. Downing remained in prison until October 7, 1907, but less than a year after gaining his freedom, he was killed in a shootout with Arizona Ranger Billy Speed at Willcox. Tomas Yoas separated from Alvord and Stiles after their jail delivery in April 1900 and was not heard of again.

Alvord remained on the run in Sonora, Mexico, until 1902 and had been worn down by the transient life of a fugitive. When he was offered a reduced sentence by Arizona Ranger Captain Burton Mossman, he was willing to listen to his proposal. Mossman met with Alvord in Mexico and agreed that if he could deliver the Graham County murderer Augustin Chacón, he would receive a sentence on the territorial charge of five years or less, and the federal charge would be dismissed. It was the best deal Alvord could hope for, so the exhausted fugitive agreed.

Stiles participated in the betrayal of Chacón and the two men delivered the Mexican to Mossman. Alvord then crossed over to Naco on September 10, 1902, and surrendered to A. V. Lewis, the sheriff of Cochise County. On December 2 the district attorney moved to dismiss the territorial charge connected with the Cochise Junction train robbery, but the federal charge, attempting to rob the U.S. mail at the Fairbanks train robbery, still stood, so Alvord was held in jail. Meanwhile Stiles, who had refused to testify at the trial against Alvord as he had agreed to do, was charged with aiding in Alvord's escape and shooting jailer Bravin. Stiles had fled to Mexico but returned seven months later and was arrested at his home, taken to the Tombstone jail, and lodged with his old partner Alvord.

On December 7, 1903, Alvord pled guilty to attempting to rob the U.S. mail and was sentenced to serve two years at the territorial prison as a federal prisoner. Alvord did not want to go to prison and Stiles was afraid to appear in court, so, ten days after Alvord's sentencing, they escaped. They cut a bar from the cell and used it to dig through the wall to freedom. Friends had left two horses saddled for them, with guns and money in the saddlebags, and they rode into Mexico.

If they had laid low, they would have succeeded in staying free, but on February 4, 1904, the two men held up John Tenner, who was transporting by wagon a $7,000 bar of gold from the weekly cleanup at the American mine near Magdalena, Sonora, Mexico. Tenner reported the matter to the Mexican authorities who, in turn, alerted American lawmen that the two robbers were probably fleeing north to avoid arrest in Mexico. On February 20, 1904, Alvord and Stiles were surprised at the "Skeets" Young ranch. In the shootout that followed, Alvord was shot in the wrist and leg with buckshot and captured, and the gold bar was recovered and returned to its owner. Stiles escaped and remained at large for several years, using the alias William Larkin. He was hired as a Humboldt County, Nevada, deputy sheriff, and in January 1908 was shot to death by the brother of a rustler he had arrested.

Alvord was taken to the Tombstone jail and watched closely until he was delivered to the territorial prison on March 14, 1904. Although the Mexican authorities filed a requisition for Alvord, he was released on October 9, 1905, without notification to the Mexican authorities. He learned of the Mexican warrant, so he fled to Panama under the alias Tom Wright, where he worked on the Panama Canal and the Madeira-Mamoré Railroad in Brazil. Soon after, he contracted yellow fever while at work on the Amazon River. On November 25, 1909, he died and was buried at the Bridgetown Cemetery.

BIBLIOGRAPHY

GENERAL REFERENCE

Block, Eugene B. *Great Train Robberies of the West*. New York: Coward-McCann Inc., 1959.

Hume, James B. and John N. Thacker. *Report: Wells, Fargo & Co.'s Express, covering a period of fourteen years*. San Francisco: H. S. Crocker and Company, 1885.

Hunter, Marvin J. And Noah H. Rose. The Album of Gunfighters. Helotes, Tex.: Warren Hunter, 1955.

Nash, Jay R. *Encyclopedia of Western Lawmen & Outlaws*. New York: Da Capo Press, 1994.

Patterson, Richard. *The Train Robbery Era, an Encyclopedic History*. Boulder, Colo.: Pruett, 1991.

Pinkerton, William A. *Train Robberies, Train Robbers and the "Holdup" Men*. New York: Arno Press, 1974.

Thrapp, Dan L. *Encyclopedia of Frontier Biography*, 3 volumes. Lincoln: University of Nebraska Press, 1988.

CHAPTER 1
THE FIRST TRAIN ROBBERY IN THE WEST

DeNevi, Don. *Western Train Robberies*. Millbrae, Calif.: Celestial Arts, 1976.

Hart, Will. "Wild West's First Train Robbery," *Wild West*, June 1998, p. 48.

McDonald, Douglas B. "The First Far-Western Train Robbery," *The West*, April 1967, p. 8.

Patterson, Richard. *Train Robbery*. Boulder, Colo.: Johnson Publishing Company, 1981.

Web sites:

http://dmla.clan.lib.nv.us/docs/nsla/archives/myth/myth55.htm.

http://www.learncalifornia.org/doc.asp?ID=112.

http://cprr.org/museum/Robbery.html.

CHAPTER 2
THE COLLINS GANG

Miller, Rick. "Bold Texas Bandit Sam Bass," *Wild West*, August 2001, p. 24.

Pearce, Bennett R. "Night of Terror at Big Springs," *Great West*, May 1971, p. 18.

Scherer, Leo. "Nebraska's Great Train Robbery," *Golden West*, January 1965, p. 14.

Spring, Agnes W. *The Cheyenne and Black Hills Stage and Express Routes*. Lincoln: University of Nebraska Press, 1948.

Wukovits, John F. "Big Score at Big Springs," *Wild West*, December 1989, p. 27.

CHAPTER 3
SAM BASS, TERROR OF THE TEXAS TRAINS

Martin, Charles L. *A Sketch of Sam Bass the Bandit*. Norman: University of Oklahoma Press, 1956.

Miller, Rick. "Bold Texas Bandit Sam Bass," *Wild West*, August 2001, p. 24.

Spring, Agnes W. *The Cheyenne and Black Hills Stage and Express Routes*. Lincoln: University of Nebraska Press, 1948.

Newspapers:

New York Times: February 24, 1878; April 12, 1878.

Web sites:

http://www.tsha.utexas.edu/handbook/online/articles/HH/egh9.html.

http://www.tsha.utexas.edu/handbook/online/articles/TT/egt8.html.

CHAPTER 4
WRECKED AND BUNGLED AT CAPE HORN

Boessenecker, John. *Badge and Buckshot: Lawlessness in Old California*. Norman: University of Oklahoma Press, 1988.

Roberts, Max. "Train Wreckers of Cape Horn." *Wild West*, August 2001, p. 32.

Newspapers:

Los Angeles Times: September 2, 1881.

San Diego Union: September 2, 1881.

San Francisco Chronicle: September 2, 1881.

CHAPTER 5
THE KIT JOY GANG

Caldwell, George A. "New Mexico's First Train Robbery," *NOLA Quarterly* XIII, 3, Winter 1989, p. 14.

Cline, Don. "Kit Joy—The One-Legged-Half-Blind-Toothless Outlaw," *NOLA Quarterly* 26, 2, April–June 2002, p. 15.

DeArment, R. K. "Sheriff Whitehill & the Kit Joy Gang," *Old West.* Winter 1994, p. 12.

Holben, Richard E. "Kit Joy's Gang," *Frontier Times.* August–September 1971, p. 20.

Newspapers:

Albuquerque Morning Journal: November 27, 1883.

New York Times: November 24, 1883.

CHAPTER 6
"GOULD'S MONEY" AND THE CORNETT-WHITLEY GANG

Burton, Jeff. "A Great Man Hunt—Correspondence from W. B. S.," *The English Westerner's Brand Book 1975–76.* London, vol. 18, 1977, p. 11.

Odell, Roy Paul. *Personal Communications.* January–February 2006.

Shults, Tommy. *Personal Communications.* January–February 2006.

Newspapers:

El Paso Daily Times: June 7, 1887; June 18, 1887.

Gonzales Inquirer: August 21, 2001.

Web sites:

http://mopac.org/history_mp.asp.

http://www.tsha.utexas.edu/handbook/online/articles/FF/hjf4.html.

CHAPTER 7
CANYON OF THE DEVIL

Barnes, William C. "The Canyon Diablo Train Robbery," *Arizona Historical Review* 3, 1, April 1930, p. 88.

Harvick, Dan. "Canyon Diablo Train Robbery," *Frontier Times*, December–January 1971, p. 8.

Kildare, Maurice. "Arizona's Great Train Robbery," *Real West*, September 1968, p. 15.

Patane, A. J. "The Diablo Canyon Holdup and the Great Chase," *Wild West*, April 2002, p. 54.

Sparks, William. *The Apache Kid, a Bear Fight . . .* Los Angeles: Skelton Publishing Company, 1926.

Walker, Dale L. "Buckey O'Neill and the Holdup at Diablo Canyon," *Real West*, November 1978, p. 40.

Newspapers:

Phoenix Herald: August 16, 1893.

Arizona Sentinel: August 19, 1893.

Web sites:

http://allhikers.com/allhikers/history/historical-figures/buckey-o'neill.htm.

CHAPTER 8
ROSCOE'S SWITCH

Boessenecker, John. *Badge and Buckshot, Lawlessness in Old California.* Norman: University of Oklahoma Press, 1988.

Edwards, Harold L. "Kid Thompson and the Roscoe Train Robberies," *True West*, January 1988, p. 48.

Kildare, Maurice. "Kid Thompson's Silver Pesos," *Westerner,* March–April 1970, p. 10.

Newspapers:

Los Angeles Times: December 25–27, 1893; February 16, 1894.

The San Diego Union: December 26, 1893.

CHAPTER 9
BLACKSTONE SWITCH

Cain, Lianne. "Texas Jack and the Blackstone Train Robbery," *True West,* January 1996, p. 14.

Reed, Nathaniel. "Train Holdup at Blackstone Switch," *The West,* May 1964, p. 16.

Shirley, Glenn. "The Bungled Job at Blackstone Switch," *True West,* May–June 1966, p. 40.

CHAPTER 10
COW CREEK CANYON

Meier, Garry and Gloria. *Oregon Outlaws.* Boise, Idaho: Tamarack Books Inc., 1996.

Newspapers

Oregonian (Portland): July 2–3, 1895; December 24, 1895.

San Francisco Chronicle: January 30, 1897; May 25, 1897.

St. Louis Globe Democrat: July 3, 1895.

CHAPTER 11
PEACH SPRINGS, ARIZONA

Edwards, Harold L. "A Rope for Cowboy Fleming Parker," *Wild West,* October 2000, p. 52.

Sharlot Hall Museum. "Statement of Love Martin's Confession." file: db 10, f.4, I.17.

Tanner, Karen H. And John D. "Parker, the Arizona Train Robber and Murderer, Hanged," *NOLA Quarterly* 26, 3, July–September 2002, p. 39.

Wilson, R. Michael. *Crime & Punishment in Early Arizona.* Las Vegas, Nev.: RaMA PRESS of Las Vegas, 2004.

Newspapers:

Arizona Journal Miner: February 9, 1897; February 17, 1897; February 24, 1897; April 28, 1897; May 7, 1897; May 12, 1897; May 15, 1897; May 17, 1897; May 26, 1897; June 2, 1897; June 8, 1897; June 11, 1897; June 17, 1897; June 23, 1897; June 30, 1897.

CHAPTER 12
THE WILD TRAIN-ROBBING BUNCH

Baker, Pearl. *Utah, 1890–1910: The Wild Bunch at Robbers' Roost.* New York: Ballantine Books, 1965.

Dullenty, Jim. "Wagner Train Robbery," *Old West.* Spring 1982, p. 40.

Ernst, Donna B. "Robbery Along the Great Northern," *True West,* June 1998, p. 46.

Ernst, Donna B. "The Wilcox Train Robbery," *Wild West,* June 1999, p. 34.

Horan, James D. *The Wild Bunch.* New York: Signet Books, 1958.

Overstreet, Charles. "A Train Robbery Turned Bad," *Old West,* Winter 1998, p. 49.

Newspapers:

New York Times: July 3, 1901; July 6, 1901; July 8, 1901; October 16, 1901.

St. Louis Globe Democrat: November 29, 1892.

CHAPTER 13
THE KETCHUM GANG

Burton, Jeffrey. "Tom Ketchum and His Gang," *Wild West*, December 2001, p. 32.

Ernst, Donna B. "A Shootout at the Turkey Creek Canyon Hideout . . . ," *Wild West*, June 1999, p. 64.

Newspapers:

Albuquerque Journal: July 20, 1898.

New Mexican: July 2, 1898; July 11–12, 1898.

Santa Fe Daily News: September 4, 1897; September 6, 1897; December 14, 1897; July 15, 1899; July 17–20, 1899; August 16–18, 1899.

Web sites:

http://pus.k12.nm.us/MSpages/Time_line/J_ritter/.

http://www.tsha.utexas.edu/handbook/online/articles/KK/fke38.html.

CHAPTER 14
COCHISE JUNCTION

Dillon, Richard. "Arizona's Last Train Robbery," *Real West*, September 1977, p. 50.

Edwards, Harold L. "Burt Alvord, the Train Robbing Constable," *Wild West*, October 2002, p. 46.

Newspapers:

Arizona Daily Citizen: February 24, 1900; April 30, 1900; May 21, 1900; June 7, 1900; June 15, 1900; June 30, 1900; July 2, 1900; July 6, 1900; July 10, 1900; December 15, 1900; December 18, 1900; May 10, 1901; December 16, 1902.

Arizona Sentinel: April 11, 1900; February 26, 1902; September 17, 1902; July 15, 1903; September 4, 1903; December 4, 1903; February 24, 1904; March 9, 1904.

Arizona Silver Belt: February 18, 1904; February 23, 1904; March 3, 1904; September 1, 1904.

Graham Guardian: December 18, 1903; January 1, 1904; February 5, 1904; February 26, 1904.

INDEX

ABOUT THE AUTHOR

R. Michael Wilson has been researching the Old West for fifteen years, following a quarter century as a law enforcement officer in Southern California. He holds an Associate Degree in Police Science, a Bachelor's Degree in Criminology, a Master's Degree in Public Administration, and a Juris Doctorate degree.

R. Michael is an active member of the National Outlaw Lawman Association (NOLA) and Western Writers of America (WWA). He has five history books to his credit, all in his area of interest and expertise—crime and punishment in America's early West. His works represent his writing philosophy: "The truth, the whole truth, and nothing but the truth."